Human Capitalism

Brink Lindsey

Human Capitalism

How Economic Growth Has Made Us Smarter—

and More Unequal

PRINCETON UNIVERSITY PRESS

Princeton and Oxford

Library of Congress Cataloging-in-Publication Data

Lindsey, Brink.
  Human capitalism : how economic growth has made us smarter-and more
unequal / Brink Lindsey.
    pages   cm
  Includes bibliographical references and index.
  ISBN 978-0-691-15732-0 (hardcover : alk. paper) 1. Economic development—
Social aspects. 2. Cognition and culture—Economic aspects. 3. Capitalism—
Social aspects. 4. Economics—Sociological aspects. I. Title.
  HD75.L564 2013
  330.12′2—dc23

                                                          2013001637

British Library Cataloging-in-Publication Data is available

This book has been composed in Minion and Helvetica

Printed on acid-free paper. ∞

Printed in the United States of America

10 9 8 7 6 5 4 3 2 1

Contents

Acknowledgments

First and foremost, I want to express deep gratitude to Bob Litan, my former colleague at the Kauffman Foundation, for believing in this book, giving me the time and freedom to write it, and offering guidance and useful feedback along the way. Thanks also to Seth Ditchik, my editor at Princeton University Press, for all his support and assistance. Eric Brynjolfsson, Bryan Caplan, Sallie James, Reihan Salam, Julian Sanchez, Dane Stangler, Steve Teles, Ben Wildavsky, and Scott Winship read drafts of the manuscript and offered incisive comments that greatly improved the final product. They are, of course, absolved from responsibility for all errors and shortcomings that remain.

Introduction

"Things were so much simpler back then . . ."

If you've reached a certain age—your forties? thirties? twenties?—you've doubtless uttered this familiar, plaintive refrain at some point.

And you were right. Because the fact is—and it's an extremely important fact—our world is getting more and more complicated all the time.

There are many reasons, but economic growth is the biggest. Growth means a more far-flung, more intricate, more highly specialized division of labor. It means continued additions to the immense accumulation of knowledge and know-how dispersed throughout society. And it means proliferating choices along virtually every dimension of human existence. Put all that together and you get one of the defining characteristics of contemporary America: its overwhelming, incomprehensible complexity.[1]

The rise in social complexity over the past century or so—basically, since industrialization took off—has pro-

1

duced a radical transformation in human experience. For one thing, it has made possible the unprecedented prosperity we now enjoy—the consequences of which I explored in a previous book.[2] Here, though, I want to look at the other side of the coin: not the effects of consuming great wealth, but the causes of our ability to produce it all.

In particular, I want to explore the strenuous mental demands placed on us by our increasingly complex social environment. To thrive and excel in the sensory and information overload of contemporary life, we have to use our brains in ways that set us apart from most people who came before us. We are rich today not simply because our superior technology and organization have made us more productive. Our minds have become more productive as well. Challenged to keep pace with the growing complexity of the world around us, we have stretched our cognitive capabilities far beyond the prevailing norms of times past.

So far, so good. The rise of complexity has been a mighty engine of human progress—not just in our possessions but in our abilities as well. By calling on us to develop our minds in novel and immensely fertile ways, it has broadened our horizons and summoned up powers we never knew we had.

But there is more to the story than that, for it's obvious that not everybody is thriving and excelling in American society today. Despite the heaping riches that our economic system continues to pile up, millions remain trapped in a nightmare world of poverty, social exclusion, and despair. And many, many more struggle ambivalently with the fact that, despite enjoying steady gains in material comfort, their overall position in society seems increasingly marginal and insecure.

Why are the blessings of American life so unevenly distributed? Because of complexity, I will argue. It is my contention that, although things were very different in the relatively recent past, today the primary determinant of socioeconomic status is the ability to handle the mental demands of a complex social environment. If you can do that, you'll likely have ample opportunities to find and pursue a career with interesting, challenging, and rewarding work. But if you can't, you'll probably be relegated to a marginal role in the great social enterprise—where, among other downsides, you'll face a dramatically higher risk of falling into dysfunctional and self-destructive patterns of behavior. Complexity has opened a great divide between those who have mastered its requirements and those who haven't.

To put this point another way, the main determinant of who succeeds and who gets left behind in American society today is possession of human capital.[3] *Human capital*, of course, is the term economists use for commercially valuable knowledge and skills. It is widely understood that, in today's "knowledge economy," the most important assets are not plant and equipment or stocks and bonds. Rather, the most important assets are the ones we carry around in our heads.

What is less well understood is why human capital has become so important, what has made its rapid accumulation possible, and how our social structure has been altered as a consequence. As I will explain in this book, the central importance of human capital in today's economy is a response to the rise of social complexity. Because it turns out that the most important forms of human capital consist of mental strategies for coping with complexity—special skills that allow us to make sense of the blooming, buzzing confusion around us, form and sustain useful relationships in a world of anonymous strangers, and impose coherence on our unruly, conflicting impulses and desires.

At the core of this book, then, is a claim about the relationship between economic development and cognitive development. Here's the basic dynamic: economic growth breeds complexity, complexity imposes increasingly heavy demands on our mental capabilities, and people respond by making progressively greater investments in human capital. As a result, capitalism has morphed into "human capitalism"—a social system in which status and achievement hinge largely on possessing the right knowledge and skills.

Over the past generation, though, the structure of American society under human capitalism has grown increasingly lopsided. And that is because the relationship between economic development and cognitive development has broken down for large sections of the population. For those in the upper third or so of the socioeconomic scale, the virtuous circle continues: increasing complexity has led to greater investments in human capital and widening opportunities for putting those investments to productive use. The rest of America, though, is being left behind: human capital levels are stagnating, and so are economic prospects.

This state of affairs is unstable. In any game where most of the players feel they are on the losing end, and where the players themselves have the power to rewrite the rules, sooner or later the pressure to change the rules will grow irresistible. For the game of human capitalism, the threat is that the rule changes will take the form of measures that undermine economic growth—and thus rising complexity, and thus the potential for the further development of human capabilities and all the social progress that such development would make possible.

What is needed instead are rule changes that expand the number of people who are able to compete and thrive in the game of human capitalism. This book concludes with a list of proposals along those lines. But first, it's necessary to explain how we got into our present situation. What is social complexity and what forces have powered its rise? How has complexity changed the way we think and work? And how has it altered the structure of society? In particular, how does it influence who gets ahead and who falls behind? To those questions we now turn.

One

The Rise of Complexity

Twenty-first-century America is a mind-boggling place. We've got more than 310 million people, 80 percent of whom are congregated in densely populated urban areas. In the business sector, more than twenty-seven million different firms compete and cooperate to supply a bewildering variety of goods and services—the typical supermarket alone stocks some thirty thousand different items. Another 1.5 million registered nonprofits, along with countless informal groups, collaborate to serve an immense range of perceived community needs. And providing the nation's legal and regulatory framework, as well as a host of other public services, are the vast bureaucracies of the federal government, fifty state governments, and more than eighty-seven thousand local governmental units. This incredibly intricate division of labor, meanwhile, is deeply integrated into a larger global economy that encompasses billions of people.

All of this highly organized, highly specialized activity requires the accumulation and communication of vast amounts of knowledge and know-how. In just the past year, nearly 248,000 new patents were granted in this country and almost 290,000 new book titles and editions were published. According to a 2003 estimate (which doubtless is already completely obsolete), the total amount of new information stored on paper, film, and magnetic and optical media in the United States comes to two trillion megabytes annually—or the equivalent of nearly fifteen thousand new book collections as big as the Library of Congress.[1] What about flows of information? Every day, Americans send six hundred million pieces of mail, make billions of phone calls, send billions more text messages, and transmit untold tens of billions of e-mails. And they spend an incredible eight hours of every day watching television, listening to the radio, reading, and surfing the Internet.

Living this way doesn't come naturally. From the first appearance of anatomically modern *Homo sapiens* more than one hundred thousand years ago until the advent of agriculture some ten thousand years ago, human beings lived as hunter-gatherers in roving bands that averaged about 150 members. The division of labor within these groups was extremely rudimentary, as virtually all able-bodied people worked in food production. Exchanges between groups were infrequent and often violent. The extent of human knowledge was limited to what could be retained in memory. Technology evolved glacially, changing noticeably only over the course of thousands of years.

The static world of the small, face-to-face group—that is our native home. That is the social environment in which we evolved and to which our brains are adapted. That is the setting for more than 90 percent of the human story so far.

So how on earth did we end up where we are now? Let's go back to the two dimensions of social complexity I highlighted above: the extent of the division of labor, and the amount of knowledge distributed throughout the system. It turns out that these two characteristics are interrelated. More to the point, they are mutually reinforcing. Stripped down to its bare essentials, the story of the rise of complexity is the story of a positive feedback loop in which the growth of the division of labor feeds the growth of knowledge, which in turn feeds the further growth of the division of labor—and off we go.

Here's the basic logic. The more we know collectively, the more we have to specialize in order to make effective use of that knowledge. The growth of knowledge thus creates an incentive for specialization. Specialization, meanwhile, expands our overall knowledge base. First, we learn by doing, so a wider variety of occupations leads to wider varieties of expertise. In addition, more specialists overall mean, among other things, more people who specialize in discovery and innovation.

But for most of human existence, the conditions that allow this logic to operate were absent. Namely, we just didn't know enough. Only with the advent of agriculture ten millennia ago was the critical threshold crossed. Because of the superior productivity of cultivation and animal husbandry, a food surplus emerged for the first time— which meant that some people could be liberated from food production and devote their full attention to other tasks. Specialization on a significant scale was now possible, and with it came the first cities—agglomerations of people who depend on others for food—and huge additional breakthroughs in knowledge. The most important of those was the invention of writing, which freed the accumulation of knowledge from the limits of memory and the transmission of knowledge from the need for personal contact. Humankind entered the realm of history.

Until quite recently, however, the social institutions for developing and applying useful knowledge remained extremely inefficient. Consequently, the positive feedback loop between knowledge and specialization ran slowly and suffered frequent and lengthy breakdowns. And the division of labor stayed quite limited. Outside a few relatively small cities (only rarely did the largest exceed one hundred thousand people), more than 90 percent of humanity continued to eke out a bare subsistence in small, isolated groups. Now the groups were villages of sedentary peasants rather than tribes of mobile hunter-gatherers, but the distinction made little difference. Indeed, according to the economic historian Gregory Clark, the typical peasant worked harder and experienced an even lower standard of living than did his hunter-gatherer ancestors.[2]

The critical turning point came in the past few centuries with the emergence of two new and immensely potent systems of social institutions: the modern market economy and modern science. Both relied on decentralized processes of experimentation and feedback—what came to be known as the scientific method for the one; entrepreneurial investment, competitive enterprise, and the profit-and-loss system for the other. Both utilized new methods of quantitative reasoning (calculus, for example, and double-entry bookkeeping) that enabled unprecedented degrees of analytical sophistication and rigor. Both broke free of traditional cultural constraints to pursue innovation and discovery wherever they might lead.

For some time, these two sets of institutions developed more or less independently. Indeed, many of the early advances in industrial technology were the handiwork of inspired tinkerers and entrepreneurs, not men of science. But by the middle of the nineteenth century, the two paths converged. The increasing dependence of economic production in western Europe and North America on technological innovation eventually led to the systematic application of scientific methods to technological problems—and thus to the integration of science and commerce. The result was a second quantum leap in human productivity—an advance that the Nobel Prize–winning economic historian Douglass North calls the "second economic revolution."[3]

It is this revolution, more commonly known as industrialization, that has carried us to the dizzying heights of economic abundance and social complexity we now occupy. In the industrial era, the growth of knowledge has exploded. Over the past century or so, annual technological progress, or productivity growth, has averaged 1 percent or higher in healthy advanced economies. By contrast, throughout the agrarian age, technological progress never surpassed 0.05 percent a year for any sustained period.[4] The division of labor, likewise, has undergone a radical transformation. Today, because of the rise in productivity, fewer than 2 percent of Americans work as farmers—down from nearly two-thirds in 1850. The positive feedback loop between knowledge and specialization now spins so fast that conditions change dramatically from decade to decade.

Born and raised in this vertiginous world, we take it for granted and assume it is normal. It is emphatically not normal. We are a scant few generations removed from the biggest discontinuity in human existence in ten thousand years. More changes in the human condition have occurred in this brief period than in all the more than three hundred generations of the agrarian area—which, in turn, was a period of convulsive dynamism in comparison to the more than three thousand generations of hunting and gathering that proceeded it. We are all unwitting participants in the biggest revolution of them all.

Two
The Abstract Art of Modern Living

The rise of complexity has thrust us into a social environment of vastly superhuman scale. According to the anthropologist Robin Dunbar, our brains are constructed so that we can maintain personal relationships with only about 150 people at a time—which just happens to have been the size of the typical Stone Age tribe. And today, this "Dunbar number" equals the number of names in the average address book.[1] Yet now, in addition to the "tribe" of our personal relationships, we are enmeshed in interdependence with untold millions of other people, the vast majority of whom we will never meet.

Because of its superhuman scale, the contemporary social environment is imbued with equally superhuman intelligence. According to the psychologist Thomas Landauer, human beings end up storing about 125 megabytes of visual, verbal, tactile, and musical memory by adulthood.[2] In the Stone Age tribe, in which everybody had similar experiences and knowledge, the total amount of information stored in the social environment wasn't much greater than that individual figure. By contrast, today we are able to tap into and make use of the highly differentiated contents of millions upon millions of other minds. And because of our ability to store data outside of our heads, that only scratches the surface of the knowledge we have accumulated. Recall that, according to the estimate I cited in chapter 1, Americans produce and store two trillion megabytes of new information every year. At that rate, it would take less than seven years to exceed the total contents of all the memories of all the people who have ever lived!

How do we cope with such incomprehensible complexity? How do we function in the twenty-first century with minds built for the Stone Age? Given the hardwired cognitive limits on how many people we can know and how much knowledge we can retain, we are swimming in water way over our heads. How do we stay afloat?

The key lies in our capacity for abstract thought. Abstraction is our master strategy for dealing with complexity. Broad conceptual categories and general rules provide the mental shortcuts we need to handle a more complex environment. To extend our knowledge beyond the range of our perception. To interact successfully with more people than we can possibly know personally. To formulate and execute plans that reach far beyond the immediate satisfaction of basic appetites.

Of course, a capacity for conceptual thinking and rule-following has been with humanity from the beginning. But until quite recently, most people did little to develop that capacity—for the simple reason that nothing in the way they lived called on them to do so. In the formative setting of the Stone Age tribe, what mattered was the concrete, the tangible, and the here and now. You survived on the basis of specific, detailed knowledge of the resources and dangers present in your local environment. Virtually the only people you ever dealt with were those you knew personally, many of whom were related to you. Time horizons did not extend beyond daily routines and the cycle of the seasons. And just about everything you did was scripted in advance by specific rituals and traditions.

The rise of social complexity has triggered an associated rise of abstract thinking. The only way to make sense of our increasingly complicated surroundings has been to broaden the conceptual categories we use. Consequently, the focus of our thoughts and decisions has shifted away from specific, tangible things and toward larger, more general classes of objects or phenomena. This turn toward the abstract has affected not only the way we understand the physical world around us but also how we conceive of our relationships with other people and our own internal desires and motivations.

Let's start with what is arguably *the* most fundamental of abstract reasoning skills: literacy. While human beings may possess an inborn "language instinct," they possess no equivalent instinct for reading and writing. Literacy requires sustained, conscious effort to master an abstract code of phonetic and punctuation symbols. And with literacy comes access to a much larger vocabulary and more complex grammar than exist in languages that are only spoken. Learning to read and write thus requires the development of highly refined abstract analytical skills; in turn, the ability to read and write creates a platform for the further development of those skills.

Throughout the agrarian era, literacy was the exclusive possession of a tiny elite of clerics and aristocrats. The world of the peasantry—the world of the small group, of concreteness and simplicity—had no need for the rarefied talents of reading and writing. But with industrialization came a growing demand for workers who could handle more complex tasks and a more highly structured lifestyle. A growing demand, in other words, for people who could read and write. As of 1800, only about 15 percent of people worldwide had achieved basic literacy; today the figure is more than 80 percent. In the more advanced United States, the literacy rate in 1800 was already 60 percent; by 1890, it had surpassed 90 percent.[3]

A similar story can be told with numeracy. For a glimpse into the possible workings of the primeval mind, consider the modern-day hunter-gatherers of the Amazonian Pirahã tribe. They don't know how to count, as the only three quantitative words in their language translate roughly into "one," "two," and "many." Even in historical time, a general haziness about numbers was pervasive until comparatively recently. Thus, studies of Roman tombstones show that incorrect ages were given about half the time; a similar absence of age awareness shows up in medieval records.[4]

Logical reasoning and abstract problem-solving skills have also improved dramatically. People have always been able to make deductions and classify things into categories, but in the past those abilities were rooted in the specific facts of everyday life. The idea of using abstractions and logic in a purely formal way—that is, regardless of the underlying subject matter—was utterly foreign. For example, in a series of interviews with Soviet peasants during the

1930s, the psychologist Alexander Luria documented a startling resistance to thinking logically about unfamiliar situations. In one instance, an illiterate peasant named Nazir-Said was presented with the following syllogism: "There are no camels in Germany. The city of B. is in Germany. Are there camels there or not?" Nazir-Said replied, "I don't know; I've never seen German villages." When the syllogism was repeated, the peasant offered, "Probably there are camels there." Pressed further, he said, "If it's a large city, there should be camels there." Luria kept trying, but to no avail.[5]

The trend in IQ scores over the course of the past century shows a striking change in mental abilities. I'm talking here about the remarkable and puzzling "Flynn effect"—the whopping rise in raw IQ scores that has now been documented in dozens of countries. According to the psychologist Ulric Neisser, if American children in 1932 could somehow have taken an IQ test normed in 1997, their average IQ score would have been around 80.[6] In other words, half the children in 1932 would have been classified as borderline retarded or worse according to 1997 standards!

Nobody believes that conclusion is correct, so what's going on? If you look at the various subtests that factor into an overall IQ score, you'll see that the raw scores in many of them have increased only modestly or not at all. It turns out that the Flynn effect is heavily concentrated in certain kinds of cognitive skills—in particular, the most abstract kinds of reasoning and problem-solving abilities. That clue suggests that the Flynn effect is being driven by social complexity. Just as the changing social environment has triggered dramatic improvements in literacy and numeracy, it has done the same with abstract analytical skills. As our external surroundings grow more complex, so do the internal structures of our thoughts.

Our increasing reliance on abstraction isn't limited to our intellectual lives. Our social lives and our internal emotional lives have also been profoundly affected. The interpersonal dimension of modern life involves highly complex interactions with large numbers of people under a wide variety of different circumstances. The intrapersonal dimension, meanwhile, involves an incessant barrage of choices that range from the most trivial to the most profound. In both cases, the mental demands of effective functioning far exceed anything our ancestors faced.

As social animals, human beings are hardwired to think of themselves as members of groups—and to feel a special sense of obligation to fellow members. Until the rise of complexity, however, most people had extremely concrete—and therefore narrow—conceptions of group identity. As a result, their capacities for trust and mutually beneficial cooperation could operate only within tightly circumscribed boundaries.

In humanity's primeval setting, there was only one group—the tribe—and the distinction between "us" and "them" was stark indeed. Contrary to romantic fantasies about noble savages, the evidence now suggests that intergroup interaction in the prehistoric era was unremittingly violent. According to the anthropologist Lawrence Keeley, about 0.5 percent of the population died every year from warfare.[7] To put that modest-sounding figure in perspective, consider the fact that about one hundred million people died in the bloody wars of the twentieth century. Had the prehistoric mortality rate still prevailed, however, the death toll would have been two billion!

Peasant life was considerably less violent but only modestly less insular. Most people spent their entire lives in a single village, rarely traveling more than a few miles from where they were born. Social bonds, accordingly, were based on concrete connections: common blood, common soil. In its bleakest form, the peasant ethos descended into what the sociologist Edward Banfield, in his landmark study of southern Italy, called "amoral familism." Its guiding precept, according to Banfield: "Maximize the material, short-run advantage of the nuclear family; assume that all others will do likewise."[8] Here, the actual war of all against all had been replaced by a kind of cold war of fear and suspicion. Elsewhere the extended family often served to broaden the circle of affections and permit a more expansive sense of community. Yet even so, the circle never extended far. The world outside the village was mysterious and vaguely menacing.

Now, of course, things are very different. In today's highly complex social order, group identity has broken free from the concrete connections of kinship, place, and long-time personal familiarity. Most of the teeming multiplicity of contemporary social bonds are based on abstractions: common values, common interests, and common expectations about the many and varied roles we assume over the course of a day. In the workplace, in shops, and on the street, we interact with large numbers of people whom we don't know, or don't know well, as concrete individuals. Instead, we know them only or primarily as members of abstract categories: commuters, pedestrians, coworkers, suppliers, customers, salespeople, doctors, police officers, and so on. We are able to get along and cooperate with them by making one leap of abstraction after another: matching the proper category to the relevant context and playing our part according to the rules and standards that govern that category of relationship.[9]

These roles we play are "thin" identities: they leave out most of the rich detail of our personalities and life histories. Consequently, spending too much time in these roles can feel hollow and unsatisfying. But it is precisely because these identities are so incomplete that we can master such a wide variety of them, and thus interact with so many different people in so many different ways. Meanwhile, we still maintain personal lives in which our "thick" identities are fully engaged. Yet even here, in our most intimate and meaningful relationships, the turn to the abstract has been transformative. Loves and friendships are increasingly rooted, not in common biographical details, but in shared outlooks and affinities and goals. In other words, we are attracted to one another's abstractions.

How do we manage all these proliferating social identities? And how do we pursue our abstract goals and achieve our abstract values? We are able to meet these challenges by virtue of a revolution in personal identity. Until the rise of complexity, most people's identities were embedded in fixed and concrete traditions. The individual was all but submerged in the group, and the range of discretion in determining the course of one's life was extremely narrow. In today's complex social environment, by contrast, people are called on to exercise autonomy—to lead self-directed as opposed to tradition-directed lives. This fundamental shift can also be seen as a shift in temporal orientation: from a life rooted in a remembered past to one focused on an imagined future.

For our hunter-gatherer and peasant ancestors, the group identity in which they were raised was the only reality they knew. You inherited a particular way of life and that was that: you lived the same as your parents did and their parents before that. The idea that the future could be different, and that you could take actions to make it so, was all but unimaginable. Edward Banfield caught a glimpse of this fatalistic mentality when he asked a southern Italian peasant woman named Laura why some people in her region were rich and others poor. Clearly flummoxed, Laura replied, "Who knows about things which have to do with the creation of the world?"[10]

With complexity, though, has come the individuation of personal identity. People now do widely differing things, and know widely differing things, and therefore their individual perspectives diverge in countless unique directions. Meanwhile, the choices confronting all these distinctive individuals have exploded as well. Under these conditions, it is no longer possible for a common set of concrete dos and don'ts to guide people through their lives. To keep up with complexity, people must learn to make their own way by their own lights.

Which means you must learn to live in the future. If you're trying to decide between specific courses of action, you need to be able to conceive of alternative, hypothetical futures in order to weigh the actions' respective consequences. To come up with possible courses of action, you need to be able to envision a future in which your goals have been advanced and your values vindicated, and your vision of the future has to be clear enough and realistic enough that you can tell how to get there from here. Through all the choices you face, from the quotidian to the life-altering, you need to be able to factor the interests and needs of an imagined future self into your decision making. All of which requires impressive feats of abstract analysis and reasoning.

A key indicator of a person's degree of future orientation is his time preference—that is, the extent to which he prefers good things right now to good things at some point in the future. If you consider the future to be inscrutable and beyond your control, your time preference is likely to be high. You'll want to grab the bird in the hand, and you'll discount sharply the prospect of future rewards. If, on the other hand, you're used to making long-term plans and seeing them come to fruition, your time preference will probably be lower. You'll be more willing to trade off gains in the present for bigger gains down the road.

Anthropological and historical evidence confirms that time preferences used to be much higher. The Pirahã tribespeople—the ones who don't know how to count—display virtually no interest in future events, and other existing hunter-gatherer societies behave similarly. And according to Gregory Clark, time preferences were also higher in the agrarian age than today. Rates of return on capital stood at 10 percent or higher in ancient and medieval times, but had fallen to 4–5 percent by the outset of industrialization. He argues persuasively that the change occurred, not because of a fall in the riskiness of investments, but because of declining time preference.[11] In the modern era, as we spend more and more time thinking about the future, it has grown increasingly real and distinct to us. Accordingly, we've grown more comfortable with deferring gratification to advance our long-term interests.

The abstract art of modern living thus has three distinctive dimensions. *Intellectual abstraction* allows us to make sense of the world around us through the use of broad concepts, symbols, and formal reasoning. *Social abstraction* enables us to interact constructively with strangers by way of a highly elaborate game of role playing. And *personal abstraction* empowers us to exercise meaningful autonomy through weighing how various choices will affect an imagined future self. Together, these three dimensions of abstraction have made it possible for human beings to operate in the strange and highly artificial world of modern social complexity. Just how at home we feel in this world, and how well we are able to satisfy its arcane and intricate demands, turn ultimately on our overall fluency with this new style of thinking—as we shall see in the next chapter.

Three
Capitalism with a Human Face

The mutually reinforcing interplay between economic development and cognitive development has had profound implications for the structure of American society. Who gets ahead, who struggles to keep up, and who gets left behind are now determined primarily by how people cope with the mental challenges of complexity. And the stakes have risen considerably in recent decades as the distance between society's winners and everybody else has widened.

Capitalism was Marx's term for the social system dominated by the owners of physical capital—the plant, machinery, and equipment that at that time constituted the rising industrial economy's "means of production." That system, though, has given way to one in which human capital is now the dominant form of wealth. According to the Nobel Prize–winning economist Gary Becker, some 70 percent of all the capital in the United States today consists of investments in health, knowledge, and skills.[1] It therefore makes sense to call our current social system human capitalism.

Thriving in this system hinges largely on possession of human capital. And the most critical forms of human capital are the capacities for intellectual, social, and personal abstraction that allow us to cope with our complex social environment.

When economists trace the linkages between human capital and socioeconomic achievement, they identify the following three forms of human capital as especially important: (1) cognitive ability as measured by standardized intelligence tests; (2) "noncognitive skills" such as motivation, perseverance, and sociability; and (3) college and graduate education.

Although raw brainpower alone is no guarantee of worldly success, the fact is that most well-paying, high-status occupations realistically are open only to those who surpass certain IQ thresholds. With a median score of 100, you have the intellectual capability to finish high school and maybe community college, but obtaining a four-year degree is probably going to be a stretch. Accordingly, all the higher-level jobs for which that degree is now a prerequisite are likely out of reach. Scores of 115, a full standard deviation above the median, are much more typical of college graduates who go on to become managers and professionals. Meanwhile, with a score of 85, or a standard deviation below the median, finishing high school may well be a challenge, and consequently only the lower rungs of the career ladder will likely be reachable.[2]

Most of us know brilliant people whose lives never fulfilled their early promise, and also overachievers whose considerable accomplishments have come more from hard work and dedication than from any native talent. The findings of social science corroborate our experience and confirm our commonsense judgment: you need both brains and a good attitude to get ahead, and a surplus of the latter can compensate for a deficit of the former. Consider the Nobel Prize–winning economist James Heckman's striking studies of the General Education Development (GED) test. Heckman has found that the earnings of high school dropouts who go on to obtain a GED certificate resemble those of other dropouts, not those of students who actually earned a high school diploma. Heckman concludes that although GED holders are comparable in intelligence to high school grads who don't go to college, their shortcomings in "noncognitive" skills—motivation, dependability, perseverance—end up dragging them down.[3]

The clearest single dividing line in America today when it comes to socioeconomic status is the distinction between those who do and don't possess a college degree. First of all, college graduates make more money—70 percent more, on average, than people with only a high school diploma, up from 30 percent more back in 1980.[4] Not only do their jobs pay better but they're more secure as well. The unemployment rate for college grads is typically much lower than that for everybody else. College graduates also enjoy greater stability in their family lives. Take single motherhood: only about 4 percent of moms with college degrees have never been married, as opposed to 15 percent of moms who graduated from high school and 25 percent of those who dropped out.[5] In addition, divorce rates are much lower among college grads. The well-educated are healthier as well. They exercise more, smoke much less, and are less likely to be obese than their fellow citizens. And they're more involved in their communities. Americans with college degrees are dramatically less likely to be behind bars, they vote more regularly, and they devote more time to volunteer work.[6]

Once you start looking at success in the social arena from the perspective of keeping up with complexity, the importance of these particular types of human capital makes perfect sense. Of course cognitive ability or measured IQ matters a lot, since what's being measured are reading, math, and formal reasoning skills—what I call fluency with intellectual abstraction. Likewise, consider "noncognitive skills"—although the term is a misnomer, as all of them generally contain an element of abstract cognition. Traits like motivation and perseverance fall under what I call personal abstraction, while one crucial component of "people skills" is the ability to recognize connections with people from varying backgrounds and perspectives—in other words, fluency with social abstraction. High academic achievement, meanwhile, depends on a combination of all three kinds of fluency with abstraction: not only "book smarts," but also long time horizons and the ability to make your way through bureaucratic institutions.

Let me concede right now that not all human capital can be boiled down to fluency with abstraction. Good looks, personal charm, a sense of humor, musical or athletic or artistic ability—these kinds of physical or personality traits are all forms of human capital that can help to propel a person into the socioeconomic elite. Even so, developing such nonintellectual talents and deploying them successfully in a workplace setting almost always requires, or at least is greatly aided by, high motivation, organization, and planning. Thus, fluency with abstraction is *the* generic form of human capital—the master strategy for coping with a complex social environment.

In its broad outlines if not in every detail, the country's social structure is now organized around the ability to handle complexity. We usually picture society as a pyramid, with the "lower" class at the bottom and the "upper" class at the exclusive apex. But for present purposes, it's better to think horizontally rather than vertically: core versus periphery instead of top versus bottom.

At the dense central core of the structure sits the socioeconomic elite of managers, professionals, and entrepreneurs. Here is where things are most complicated: more information is processed, bigger pictures are seen and overseen, and therefore more highly abstract thinking of one kind or another is needed. Here the members of the elite earn society's highest material, psychic, and status rewards by directing, coordinating, and analyzing the headspinning intricacies of twenty-first-century life. Most have successfully completed long years of formal training in school. They tend to be good at analytical reasoning, organization, and follow-through. Building social networks and navigating through the twists and turns of bureaucratic procedures are second nature to them. They have motivations and expectations that keep the long term always in view. In sum, they are flush with human capital—which is to say, they excel at coping with complexity. Deploying these assets, they occupy the nation's centers of power and influence.

On the widely scattered periphery, meanwhile, are the members of the working class. They lack extensive schooling and have not done much otherwise to invest in developing marketable skills. They are less adroit at dealing with big, impersonal institutions. Their time horizons don't extend as far into the future. They are, in sum, less well adapted to social complexity. Most jobs performed by blue-collar and service workers are relatively simple and routine, and they offer only limited scope for advancement. The need for analytical problem solving, organizational sophistication, long-term planning, and personal initiative is correspondingly modest.

Between the core and the periphery are the middle ranks of office workers and salespeople. The complexity of their work, as well as their socioeconomic status, occupies an intermediate position between that of the elite and that of the working class. And beyond the periphery, on the fringes of social life, is the chaos of poverty. People trapped here contribute productively to the economy only haphazardly or not at all.

With the emergence of human capitalism has come a dramatic expansion in opportunities for people to develop their talents and flourish accordingly. Consider, first of all, the phenomenal rise in levels of education. Back in 1900, the ratio of new high school graduates to seventeen-year-olds was only 6 percent; the ratio reached 70 percent by 1960, and has fluctuated around there ever since. The boom in high school education during the first half of the century was matched by a college boom in the second half. As of 1950, only 8 percent of Americans between the ages of twenty-five and twenty-nine had a college degree; by 1980, that figure had risen to 23 percent.

Opportunities for interesting, challenging work in safe and comfortable settings have multiplied as well. Back in 1900, 79 percent of the workforce were employed as farmers, manual laborers, or domestic servants. Today, by contrast, 60 percent of workers hold white-collar office jobs. Especially noteworthy is the process that the University of Chicago economist Frank Knight, writing presciently back in the 1920s, referred to as the "cephalization" of economic life.[7] Just as, when animals evolve to be capable of more complex behaviors, their brain-to-body ratios keep increasing, so our economy's "brain"—its managerial, professional, and entrepreneurial elite—keeps getting relatively bigger as well. Managerial and professional occupations made up only about 10 percent of the workforce in 1900, whereas they make up some 35 percent today. In other words, the American economy's "brain-to-body ratio" has more than tripled—and the demand for highly skilled "knowledge workers" has shot up accordingly.

This increasing demand for human capital has helped to undermine old barriers to social mobility. In the first half of the twentieth century, the socioeconomic elite was much smaller than today's, and its work was less demanding. As a result, the number of people capable of serving in elite occupations was considerably larger than the number of available positions. In that world, access to the elite had relatively less to do with ability and relatively more to do with gender, skin color, and surname—in other words, membership in the proverbial old boys' network. Large numbers of otherwise qualified people were excluded from high-paying, high-status careers on the basis of race, sex, religion, and pedigree. While family connections and discrimination continue to influence social position, the strong economic imperative to find and make use of talent has pushed the country in a decidedly meritocratic direction.

Although the social progress unleashed by human capitalism has been breathtaking, it has also been uneven. Old structural barriers to human flourishing rooted in racism and sexism may have weakened, but class-based barriers have been rising in their stead. In subsequent chapters I'll offer an explanation of how this happened and what might be done about it, but next I want to examine the nature of those barriers. We've already seen that in contemporary American society, a person's level of human capital is a major determinant of her socioeconomic status. It turns out, though, that causation runs in the other direction as well. That is to say, the socioeconomic status into which a person is born has a huge impact on how much human capital he will ultimately amass.

Four
Class and Consciousness

In the previous chapter we saw that economic life today is organized around differences in human capital—in particular, different capacities for dealing with complexity. The occupations that provide the highest pay and status are, in general, the ones that handle society's most complex and cognitively demanding tasks, and thus the socioeconomic elite consists of people who are good at performing these kinds of tasks. The less adept you are at coping with complexity, the humbler your position in the social hierarchy is likely to be.

All of which raises the question: what determines who is rich in human capital and who is poor? In other words, why is human capital so unevenly distributed?

Once you understand human capital in terms of fluency with abstraction, and once you see that fluency with abstraction is a learned response to the rise of social complexity, you're ready to solve a big part of the puzzle. Specifically, a major contributor to human capital inequality lies in the chicken-and-egg relationship between economic class and cognitive culture.

The key, relevant insight here is this: our increasing facility with abstract thought represents a cultural adaptation to changes in our social environment. Because of the complex tasks we will be called on to handle as adults, we are taught new mental skills in childhood that our forebears never had reason to learn—skills that we continue to develop throughout adulthood. The mechanism for transmitting these skills from one generation to the next is culture—the web of norms, values, and beliefs that creates a shared way of life.

We should therefore expect to find an association between the relative complexity of the social environment in which people are raised as children and live as adults and the degree of cultural adaptation that they exhibit. And that is precisely what we do find in American society today. Specifically, working-class families and communities have a culture different from that of managerial and professional families and communities—one that is much less oriented toward encouraging and reinforcing the abstract thinking needed to master complexity.

Sociologists have understood this for a long time. Consider the classic work by Herbert Gans, *The Urban Villagers*, an in-depth study of working-class Italian Americans in Boston's West End during the 1950s. Gans described the culture he encountered as a "peer group society" in which people's identities and aspirations were inextricably connected to a specific circle of family members and friends from childhood. The larger society in which they lived existed in their imaginations as a somewhat mysterious and often hostile "them." "The West Ender always expects to be exploited in his contact with the outside world," Gans wrote, "and is ready to exploit it in return."[1] In other words, Gans saw that West Enders lacked a highly developed capacity for social abstraction—the ability to move in and out of various chosen "thin" identities and play those roles with an ever-changing cast of acquaintances and strangers.

In her study of middle-class, working-class, and poor families titled *Unequal Childhoods*, the sociologist Annette Lareau has corroborated Gans's analysis in key respects. On the one hand, she finds that kin relationships are much closer and more important for working-class and poor families than for their middle-class counterparts. On the other hand, in dealing with authorities and institutions outside the family circle, "middle-class family members appeared reasonably comfortable and entitled, while working-class and poor families appeared uncomfortable and constrained."[2]

Gans characterized the working-class inhabitants of the West End as "person-oriented" in their goals, in contrast to the "object-oriented" striving of middle-class life. What did he mean by an "object"? "This may be a moral object, for example, a principle," he wrote; "an ideological object, such as 'understanding'; a material object, such as level of income; a cultural object, such as a style of life; or a social object, such as a career or a status position."[3] Gans's concept of object-orientation is thus the equivalent of what I have called personal abstraction: the future-oriented formulation and pursuit of abstract goals.

By contrast, the person-oriented striving that Gans observed in the West End related to the much more concrete goal of fitting in and enjoying life within the confines of a given peer group. "West Enders, for example, are not interested in careers, but in jobs that pay the most money for the least amount of physical discomfort, because they want to make money and save their energy for person-oriented behavior within the peer group," Gans wrote. "Similarly, they do not strive to live up to moral or ideological principles, but want to act in a way that earns no opprobrium from the group, and fits group beliefs."[4]

The relative absence of abstract life goals translates into a relative absence of future orientation—and, consequently, an approach to morality and self-discipline that differs sharply from the middle-class way of life. Middle-class people tend to govern their desires and curb their appetites through a relatively flexible and customized process of making trade-offs: they balance the short-term needs and wants of their present selves against the long-term interests of their imagined future selves. By contrast, members of the working class are less likely to make the interests of a hypothetical future self a compelling factor in decision making. Consequently, they tend to rely more heavily on external reinforcement—in particular, the opinions of friends, family members, and specific authority figures like priests—to keep their lives in order.

Let's turn now to the third dimension of the abstract art of modern living: intellectual abstraction. Here again, class distinctions have important implications for the way people think—in particular, how they use language. In the early 1970s, the British sociologist Basil Bernstein introduced the concept of "restricted" and "elaborated" language codes, or styles of communication. Restricted codes assume the existence of considerable shared knowledge within a group; consequently, relatively few words are needed to convey meaning. By contrast, elaborated codes spell everything out in explicit detail so that people from all kinds of different backgrounds can still communicate effectively with one another. According to Bernstein, members of the working class tend to use restricted language codes exclusively, while middle-class people flip back and forth between restricted codes with family and friends and an elaborated code for the wider world.[5] This pattern accords with Gans's and Lareau's observations about working-class rootedness in a specific peer group and alienation from the larger society.

But if different approaches to the use of language grow out of different capacities for social abstraction, they in turn have a profound effect on capacities for reasoning and analytical thinking—that is, intellectual abstraction. As Annette Lareau has noted, middle-class families "use language as an end in and of itself. They enjoy words for their own sake, ascribing an intrinsic pleasure to them." For the working-class and poor families that Lareau observed, on the other hand, "language serves as a practical conduit of daily life, not as a tool for cultivating reasoning skills or a resource to plumb for ways to express feelings or ideas."[6]

The cultural differences between socioeconomic classes are perpetuated from generation to generation. Although the fact flies in the face of cherished myths about American society, it turns out that the surest path to becoming a well-educated, high-performing member of the socioeconomic elite is to pick the right parents. In this fabled land of opportunity, it has long been the conventional wisdom that the advantages of family background are modest and fleeting—hence the old saying about "shirtsleeves to shirtsleeves in three generations." And until recently, economists largely agreed with the popular view. However, improved

techniques of tracking socioeconomic status across generations now show that social mobility is considerably weaker
than previously believed. People raised in the upper middle class are far more likely to stay there than move down,
while people raised in the working class are far more likely
to stay there than move up.[7] Specifically, according to research from the Brookings Institution, a child born in the
bottom quintile of income has only a 17 percent chance of
winding up in the top 40 percent of income, while a child
born in the top quintile has only a 24 percent chance of
dropping down to the bottom 40 percent.[8]

This state of affairs may be dispiriting, but it shouldn't
be too surprising. The more complex our society becomes,
the further removed it is from the ancestral environment
in which our brains evolved. Which means, the more challenging the task of training our minds to cope with what's
going on around us. So if you want to raise a middle-class,
college-educated knowledge worker, you need to get started
as soon as possible, and you need to keep at it unrelent-
ingly. Accordingly, it makes sense that the children of the
socioeconomic elite, immersed since birth in a culture of
complexity, are the ones best positioned to adapt most successfully. By contrast, children of the working class and the
poor are raised in environments much less conducive to developing the capacities for abstract living.

Thanks to Malcolm Gladwell's best-selling *Outliers*, many
of us are now familiar with the "10,000 hour rule": in almost any field you can think of, you can't perform at the very
highest level without logging the requisite hours of diligent,
focused practice.[9] Gladwell was relying on the findings of
the so-called Expert Performance Movement, led by the psy-

chologist Anders Ericsson. In their systematic study of elite performers in a wide variety of fields, Ericsson and fellow researchers have come to the conclusion that "natural talent" is a will-o'-the-wisp. According to their research, what distinguishes superstars from the rest of the field is that they started at a younger age and trained more hours a day over a period of many years. Sheer volume of "deliberate practice" is the key in their view: not mere repetition, but the effortful pursuit of mastery with concrete goals and constant adjustment of techniques based on careful evaluation of results.

When it comes to acquiring human capital—that is, developing expertise in coping with complexity—children of the socioeconomic elite are similarly distinguished from their less advantaged peers. By the time they start school, they already have a huge head start in developing the cognitive skills needed to achieve high performance in the social arena. And throughout their years of schooling, which typically will extend through college or even graduate school, they tend to pull ever further ahead, thanks to unremitting encouragement and reinforcement from those around them.

A growing body of psychological and sociological research confirms the crucial importance of the child-rearing environment. For example, the child psychologists Betty Hart and Todd Risley estimate that by the time they reach age three, children of professional parents have heard some forty-five million words addressed to them—as opposed to only twenty-six million words for working-class kids, and a mere thirteen million words in the case of kids on welfare. Unsurprisingly, the upper-middle-class toddlers they observed had average vocabularies of 1,176 words, while the working-class and welfare kids averaged 749 and 525 words, respectively.[10]

Meanwhile, Annette Lareau has identified clear class differences in parenting styles. Working-class parents, she observes, continue to follow the traditional, laissez-faire child-rearing philosophy that she calls "the accomplishment of natural growth." At the upper end of the socioeconomic scale, though, parents now engage in what she refers to as "concerted cultivation"—intensively overseeing kids' schoolwork and stuffing their after-school hours and weekends with organized enrichment activities. As a result of the more intensive parental involvement, more advantaged kids work harder in school, have much more practice managing their time, and develop greater self-assurance in dealing with new social situations.[11]

In her provocative and widely discussed book *The Nurture Assumption*, the psychologist Judith Rich Harris argues that peer groups have a much greater influence on a child's development than do parents.[12] It's a controversial thesis, but for present purposes it's a moot question: when it comes to class-based differences in human capital formation, parental and peer influences tend to push in the same direction. The children of college-educated professional parents tend to hang out with one another, in large part because of their parents' choice of neighborhood, schools, and childhood playmates. Meanwhile, working-class and underclass kids likewise flock together because they live near one another and they share more experiences and attitudes. And kids on opposite sides of the class divide will naturally think very differently about the possibility and importance of doing well in school and the range of possible future careers.

Although there are certainly exceptions, for most people there is a basic continuity between the experiences of childhood and those of adult life. People who do well, or at least persevere, in meeting the complex challenges of the classroom tend to assume more complex responsibilities in the workplace. The fluency with abstraction they acquire as kids is thus reinforced and expanded throughout their working lives. And people who fail to amass much human capital during their school years seldom get the opportunity to do so as adults. Instead, they wind up in working-class jobs that do not require much fluency with abstraction. Thus, people raised in one economic class tend to remain there. Which means that, from birth to death, people in different classes are immersed in distinctly different cognitive cultures.

Class is not the only source of different cultural orientations toward complexity: ethnicity and geography are important, too, and they feed into and reinforce the effects of class. The common thread here is the degree of exposure to the peak complexities of modern life. The further, physically or socially, people are from the centers of contemporary complexity, the less their culture is likely to promote fluency with abstraction.

Rural, mountainous Appalachia is famous both for its cultural distinctiveness and its poverty, two features that of course are intertwined. And in general, rural areas are marked by lower incomes and education levels. Their position on the geographic periphery, far from the command centers of complexity, translates into location on the socioeconomic periphery as well.

African Americans and Hispanics are today disproportionately represented in the lower ranks of the socioeconomic scale, and in both cases isolation and exclusion provide the explanation. African Americans were enslaved and systematically oppressed for centuries; Hispanics immigrated here typically from poor regions of much less advanced economies. Even today, members of both groups tend to live under conditions of de facto residential segregation, and both must contend with the headwinds of adverse stereotypes commonly held among the white majority.[13]

Under these conditions, it is entirely unsurprising that cultural attitudes have arisen that reinforce these groups' marginality. A recent study by the Harvard economist Roland Fryer provides one depressing example. For the white high school students he studied, there was a positive correlation between higher grades and higher popularity. But for black and Hispanic students in integrated public schools, higher grades led to lower popularity as the high achievers were stigmatized for "acting white."

As Fryer himself points out, this kind of self-defeating behavior is not something peculiar to blacks and Hispanics. Ethnographic studies have found similar kinds of attitudes among the Buraku outcastes of Japan, the Maori in New Zealand, Italian immigrants in Boston, and the British working class.[14] It's elementary social psychology: human beings are hardwired to form self-policing social groups. With groups that are marginal to begin with, the urge to maintain group solidarity can often take the form of ostracizing anyone who appears to be forsaking the group in pursuit of mainstream success. In a less loaded example, consider the cries of "sell out" that emanate from a once-obscure band's original fan base after it hits the big time. The same dynamic plays out in class, regional, and ethnic contexts but with tragic rather than farcical results.

Five
Inequality as a Culture Gap

Making the argument that socioeconomic inequality is reinforced and perpetuated by cultural differences embroils me in a two-front war. On my right, I'm squaring off against critics who see current inequalities as rooted, not in culture, but in innate and unalterable biological differences. Genes, they say, are the dominant factor in transmitting socioeconomic advantages from one generation to the next. By contrast, differences in upbringing play at most a minor role. On my left, meanwhile, I'm taking on those who dismiss any analysis like mine as "blaming the victim." They argue instead that the real problem is a lack of resources and opportunities. In this view, there isn't much wrong with working-class culture that fatter paychecks wouldn't cure.

Let me start with the argument from genetic fatalism, the best-known version of which was made by Charles Murray and Richard Herrnstein in their controversial bestseller *The Bell Curve*. According to Murray and Herrnstein, with the breakdown of legal and social barriers against women and ethnic minorities, IQ is now the major determinant of socioeconomic success. And since, they contend, IQ differences are to a large extent inherited, there are depressingly strict limits on what can be done to improve the skill levels of the less advantaged.[1]

The specific argument made by Murray and Herrnstein can be dispensed with fairly easily for the simple reason that their focus on IQ is far too narrow. It's not just intellectual abstraction that matters: personal and social abstraction are important, too, and to a considerable extent they can compensate for a lack of intellectual firepower. Recall James Heckman's findings about the disappointing work performance of GED holders and how these results reveal the importance of "noncognitive" skills. In the same vein, a study of eighth graders by the University of Pennsylvania psychologists Angela Duckworth and Martin Seligman measured the students' self-discipline in a variety of ways. They got the students, as well as their parents and teachers, to fill out surveys that gauged how impulsive the kids were; they also administered questionnaires and behavioral tests in which students were asked to choose between a smaller reward now and a bigger delayed reward. Duckworth and Seligman found that their composite measures of self-discipline did a significantly better job of predicting the kids' grades than did IQ tests.[2]

In addition, numerous studies of the determinants of earnings have shown that all kinds of factors having nothing to do with intellectual or any other kind of abstraction play a role as well. For example, height, beauty, and self-esteem are all positively associated with labor market success. The upshot is that other factors swamp IQ when it comes to predicting socioeconomic achievement. The economists Samuel Bowles and Herbert Gintis conducted a meta-analysis of twenty-four different studies that examined the impact of IQ on earnings. Combining the direct effect of IQ with its indirect effect through schooling (more years of schooling translate into higher earnings, and higher IQ is positively correlated with more schooling), they estimate the overall effect to be 0.266—that is, a standard deviation change in IQ results in a change in earnings of a little more than one-quarter of a standard deviation. Which means that variations in IQ explain only 7 percent of variations in earnings. Further, using standard estimates for the heritability of IQ, they find that the genetic transmission of IQ accounts for only about 2 percent of the correlation between parents' and children's incomes.[3]

The evidence is thus compelling that intellectual ability alone is not the be-all and end-all of socioeconomic success. Furthermore, and more to the point that culture is at the root of class-based inequality, there are good reasons to believe that IQ is considerably more plastic than genetic fatalists like Murray and Herrnstein believe. Specifically, properly focused studies show that the socioeconomic status of the home in which a child is raised has a big impact on that child's ultimate IQ.

The best evidence that genes are destiny with respect to IQ comes from studies of twins and adopted children. Looking at identical twins raised apart holds genes constant while varying environment, whereas comparing unrelated children raised by the same adoptive parents varies genes while holding environment relatively constant. A weighted average of numerous different studies shows that the correlation between the IQ scores of identical twins raised in different homes is 0.74. By contrast, another study of unrelated kids raised in the same adoptive home shows a correlation of only 0.26. And that was a study of children. When you look at adults, correlations between the scores of unrelated siblings raised together drop to nearly zero.[4] On the basis of findings like these, it appears that genes' impact on IQ swamps that of family environment.

Not so fast, though. Taking these findings at face value assumes that the differences among adoptive families mirror those among all families generally. If it turns out, however, that adoptive families share important similarities, then the effect of family environment is going to be understated by these studies and the effect of genes correspondingly overstated. And indeed, adoptive families are distinctive—which makes sense, as couples that want to adopt are screened for fitness whereas biological parents are not. Couples that adopt tend to be better off and better educated than average, and measures of the home environment (looking at things such as how much parents talk to their kids, their affect in dealing with kids, and kids' access to books and computers) show higher overall scores and less variation in scores among adoptive families.[5]

When researchers distinguish between adoptive families based on socioeconomic status, a very different picture emerges. A study of French adopted children by the psychologists Christiane Capron and Michel Duyme was able to identify the socioeconomic status of the kids' biological as well as adoptive parents. On the one hand, the IQs of children born to high-SES parents were twelve points higher than those born to low-SES parents—a result unaffected by the adoptive parents' SES. So score one for the power of genes. On the other hand, though, the IQs of children raised in high-SES homes were twelve points higher than those raised in low-SES homes—regardless of the biological parents' SES. The implication of this finding is clear: although genes surely matter for IQ, so too does upbringing—to the tune of nearly a full standard deviation.

A similar study (also French, by the way) compared poor kids adopted into upper-middle-class families to their siblings who weren't adopted. The adopted kids received an average IQ score of 107 in one test and 111 in another; their siblings, by contrast, got an average score of around 95 on both tests. In other words, being raised in an upper-middle-class home appears to have raised children's IQ between twelve and sixteen points.[6]

These empirical findings of cultural influence on individual IQ make perfect sense once we recognize that what we call "intelligence" is itself a cultural artifact. The kinds of information stored in one's head that are considered useful, and the kinds of mental operations whose swift and effective completion brings social status and other advantages, are deeply dependent on the nature of the society into which one is born. The same mental attributes that allow someone today to sail through Ivy League schools into a high-paying professional job may, in a different time and place, be dismissed as all but useless. Thus, the idea embraced by IQ "hereditarians" that intelligence is some kind of innate physical attribute is a fundamental misconception based on ethnocentric and ahistorical thinking. What we measure on IQ tests are intellectual skills that represent a cultural adaptation to specific circumstances—namely, the novel and utterly exotic conditions of modern social complexity.

Of course there is wide individual genetic variation in the various physiological capacities that contribute to the development of fluency with intellectual abstraction. So when we note the correlation between parents' socioeconomic status and children's IQ, part of what we are seeing is surely the genetic transmission of advantageous capacities. Furthermore, the evidence does show that IQ becomes more or less fixed at around age eight, so the plasticity of IQ is quite limited compared to other attributes that contribute to socioeconomic success.[7] People continue to grow smarter after age eight in absolute terms, of course, but IQ is a relative rather than absolute measure. And it turns out your place in the intelligence bell curve gets locked in at a fairly early age.

Notwithstanding the importance of genes and the limits on plasticity, much of what we know about IQ cannot be explained without grasping that measured intelligence is a suite of learned skills that are developed, as are all skills, through extensive "deliberate practice." Which means that environment plays a crucial role in determining how well those particular skills are developed.

For example, consider the fact that the one specific intelligence test most highly correlated with overall IQ is vocabulary. Yet at both the cultural and individual level, vocabulary acquisition is primarily a function of literacy—a learned behavior that was developed quite recently in human experience and has been a mass phenomenon for only the past couple of hundred years. Looking at societies as a whole, written languages have much larger vocabularies than those used by preliterate peoples. And for the individual, a large vocabulary is acquired primarily through reading—for the simple reason that written texts utilize a vastly greater number of different words than does even relatively sophisticated oral communication.[8] The fact that what we call intelligence is so closely linked to specific and johnny-come-lately cultural practices—reading and writing—belies the notion that it is fundamentally physiological in nature.

Or take the Flynn effect, the rapid rise in raw IQ scores across the population. This striking phenomenon has occurred far too quickly to have a genetic basis. The best explanation for it is that the cultural environment for virtually everyone is growing increasingly saturated with opportunities to develop formal reasoning skills—and thus those skills are being honed to a higher level. In this regard, it's noteworthy that the Flynn effect is concentrated in particular intelligence subtests and basically nonexistent in others. Big gains are found in scores for purely abstract puzzle solving as tested in the Raven Progressive Matrices test—which makes sense, as these puzzles measure logical reasoning unmoored from any specific real-world context. Meanwhile, there has been no real rise in vocabulary scores—which again is entirely predictable since the amount of time people spend reading has been on the decline.

So much for IQ. But if we broaden our focus, there is additional evidence from twin and adoption studies that suggests that genes do dominate upbringing in explaining the intergenerational transmission of socioeconomic status. Here the objection that IQ is only a small part of the overall picture goes away, as now we are confronting the big-picture question: how important is the sum of all genetic factors in determining overall socioeconomic position? And using various simplifying assumptions, twin and adoption studies often show that genes account for most or all of the correlations among family members in income and educational attainment. Shared family environment, meanwhile, explains little or nothing.[9]

It turns out, however, that the findings from these studies are highly sensitive to the initial assumptions that are made. For example, in one study of Swedish twins, adoptees, and other siblings, the simplistic assumption that all siblings share the same similarity in family environment led to a finding that genes explain 80 percent or more of the correlation in earnings. When more realistic assumptions were made (namely, that identical twins experience a more similar environment than do other sets of siblings), the share of the correlations explained by genes dropped to roughly 60 percent.[10] Likewise, a study of Australian twins found that only 25 percent of the variation in educational attainment was due to environmental factors. But when the assumption that parents share no common genes was relaxed (to account for the known fact of "assortative mating") and measurement errors were corrected for, the share explained by environment shot up to 40 percent.[11] Furthermore, there is the previously mentioned problem that adoptive parents are not a representative sample of the overall parenting population.

Teasing through these complexities, leading scholars have come to the commonsense conclusion that nature and nurture are both important. Christopher Jencks of Harvard's Kennedy School of Government, one of the most prominent and widely respected social scientists in this field, reckons that genes account for only about 40 percent of the correlation in income between parents and children.[12] Samuel Bowles and Herbert Gintis, two other leading experts on intergenerational inequality, have estimated that genes explain about one-third of the correlations and environmental factors account for the rest.[13] Bruce Sacerdote, whose study of Korean-born adoptees in the United States shows no correlations between the incomes of adoptive parents and their children, has surveyed the broader literature and comes down firmly on both sides of the nature–nurture question. On the one hand, he notes, "economists who are not familiar with the literature are generally surprised by how much genes matter." On the other hand, "the estimated effects of family environment on adoptee outcomes are still large in some studies and leave tremendous scope for children's outcomes to be affected by family, neighborhood or school environment."[14]

Although there is at least some evidence in favor of the position, I have to agree with the psychologist Richard Nisbett when he says that the belief that family environments don't matter is "one of the most unusual notions ever accepted by highly intelligent people."[15] First, believers in genes *über alles* have to dismiss all the complexities and contrary evidence within the specific field of behavioral genetics on which they rest their whole case. Beyond that, they have to ignore all the other sources of evidence that bear on the question. As I'll discuss later, careful studies document that preschool programs and high-quality schooling can have a big impact on children's educational and broader life outcomes. How can teachers make a big difference while parents are irrelevant? In any event, both are part of the same "shared environment" that distinguishes kids raised in the elite from those raised in the working class. And as we've already seen, Anders Ericsson and his colleagues in the Expert Performance Movement have documented that the key to mastery of any skill is practice, practice, practice. So how can kids who are incessantly pushed to hone the skills associated with mastering complexity not have an advantage over those who aren't?

Perhaps the clearest evidence of the importance of cultural differences in upbringing comes from data on the assimilation of immigrant groups. In particular, second-generation immigrants (i.e., people born in the United States to foreign-born parents) typically experience big income gains relative to first-generation immigrants from the same country. For immigrants from less developed countries, this convergence toward native-born income levels is generally accompanied by big gains in relative educational attainment. Thus, according to a study by James Smith of the RAND Corporation, first-generation Mexican male immigrants born in 1940–1944 earned 65 percent of native-born white males' average lifetime earnings; second-generation immigrants born twenty-five years later (in other words, the children of the prior group) earned 82 percent of the native-born average. Meanwhile, the deficit in average years of schooling fell from 5.6 years to 1.0 years between the two generations.[16]

Nevertheless, clear differences across immigrant groups persist over time. According to George Borjas of Harvard, income differences among immigrants from any two countries of origin tend to be cut in half between the first and second generations—and then cut in half again between the second and third.[17] If those differences were big to begin with, they can remain substantial even for Americans with foreign-born grandparents.

There is no good way to make sense of either rapid "catch-up" growth in income or the long-term persistence of ethnic income differences other than by resort to cultural explanations. If genes are destiny and upbringing doesn't matter, how to explain the big jump in income? Clearly, being raised in an English-language country with better schools gives second-generation kids a big advantage over their foreign-born parents in developing the skills valued in the U.S. labor market. Meanwhile, for ethnic differences to continue into the third generation, cultural differences in parenting style and community influences must be affecting outcomes.

The fact that the genetic fatalists are wrong does not mean that human beings are infinitely malleable or that improving fluency with abstraction among broad populations is easy. Cultural inertia is a powerful force: in particular, the norms, beliefs, and habits that lead people of lower socioeconomic status to underinvest in the development of abstract thinking skills have a strong tendency to perpetuate themselves from one generation to the next. But however difficult progress is to achieve, it is not impossible.

The odds of making progress, though, are greatly enhanced by a correct understanding of the true obstacles that lie in the way. Which leads me now to pivot to the left and address those critics who dismiss cultural explanations of socioeconomic inequality as so much blaming the victim.[18] In their view, the connection between parental socioeconomic status and children's outcomes boils down to money. First, less-well-off parents can't afford the material resources needed to propel their children into college and high-paying careers. Second, the stress and inconveniences caused by lack of money consume a great deal of parents' attention that might otherwise be devoted to nurturing their kids.

These are plausible theories, but careful empirical investigation shows that they really don't add up to much. So concludes the University of Chicago sociologist Susan Mayer, whose book *What Money Can't Buy* represents the most painstakingly thorough effort to date to pin down the connection between parental income and childhood outcomes such as cognitive skills, behavior problems, teenage pregnancy, years of school completed, and wages and employment in young adulthood.

She found that conventional techniques of social-science research have tended to overstate that connection. The problem lies in the fact that many of the same characteristics that make people valuable employees (skills, motivation, reliability) also make people more effective parents. Typically researchers have tried to control for particular parental characteristics, but others are inevitably omitted. In her analysis, Mayer employed a number of ingenious strategies to weed out all extraneous factors and examine the effects of money in isolation.

For example, she compared the effects of higher wages and salaries with the effects of higher welfare payments, child support, and other non-work-related income. In addition, she probed the correlation between income and spending on the kinds of amenities associated with doing well in school (e.g., books, museum visits). She also examined whether trends in income over time matched trends in child outcomes. Through these and other means, Mayer arrived at the conclusion that "*once children's basic material needs are met*, characteristics of their parents become more important to how they turn out than anything additional money can buy."[19] The condition is emphasized for a reason. Mayer isn't suggesting that existing government programs for the poor ought to be cut. Rather, she is saying that those programs have been relatively successful at meeting kids' basic needs. Consequently, additional income redistribution is unlikely to have much impact on child outcomes.

And what are those critical parental characteristics that contribute to both career success and parenting success? You know my answer: fluency with intellectual, social, and personal abstraction. The problem does turn out to be a lack of capital—but human capital, not pecuniary capital. This kind of capital is generally acquired culturally, from family and neighborhood and peers, not in the marketplace.

I want to state categorically that there's no blame attached to my assessment of working-class culture. If society's business requires large numbers of people to spend their working lives engaged in jobs that are more physically than intellectually demanding, it is entirely appropriate and functional for those people to develop and sustain a culture that puts relatively little emphasis on cultivating analytical and organizational dexterity. What is the point of developing skills that you will not be called on to use in real life? And at the same time, if working-class jobs provide a rising standard of living for you and bright prospects for your children—as was the case in the United States for much of the twentieth century—the attractions of sticking with the lifestyle, norms, beliefs, and habits of your upbringing are obvious and considerable.

But over the past generation, changes in both working-class culture itself and the economy at large have rendered the culture gap between classes increasingly problematic. What happened and why are the subjects of the next chapter.

Six
From Convergence to Polarization

With the emergence of human capitalism in the United States during the middle decades of the twentieth century, it first appeared as if the class divisions that had plagued old-style capitalism were, if not disappearing, at least fading in significance. The postwar boom was indeed a rising tide that lifted all boats, and actually the humbler vessels were proving more buoyant than the yachts. Between 1947 and 1973, real (i.e., inflation-adjusted) income grew at an average annual rate of 3.0 percent for people in the bottom fifth of the income distribution, as opposed to 2.8 percent for those in the middle fifth and 2.5 percent for people in the top fifth.[1]

Noticing similar trends in other advanced countries, the economist Simon Kuznets proposed his eponymous curve as a general law of capitalist development. The Kuznets curve suggested a regular, inverted-U-shaped relationship between national income and inequality. During the early, messy phase of capitalist takeoff, inequality grew as physical capital powered growth and the returns redounded to a relative few, but as the main engine of growth shifted to human capital, the rewards of growth became more and more widely shared.

Yet as human capitalism reached full flower with the shift to a postindustrial, information economy, things went in a very different direction. Since the early 1970s, the inverted-U-shaped curve has given way to the "Great U-Turn"[2]—a reversal of the previous trend in which now the spread between rich and poor has been growing. Thus, between 1973 and 2001, average annual growth in real income stood at only 0.3 percent for people in the bottom fifth, compared to 0.8 percent for people in the middle fifth and 1.8 percent for those in the top fifth.[3] Similar reversals have occurred in many other advanced economies as well.

Meanwhile, poverty in America has proven depressingly persistent. Between 1959 (when the modern poverty line was first formulated) and 1973, the percentage of Americans living in poverty fell by half—from 22.4 percent to 11.1 percent. Since then, however, the poverty rate has bounced around between 11 and 15 percent, drifting upward through the 1970s, 1980s, and early 1990s, falling during the 1990s boom, and climbing back to 15.1 percent by 2010 in the wake of the Great Recession.

Economic inequality has become a highly loaded issue, and passions have been especially inflamed by the huge gains reaped in recent decades by the very highest earners. But in my view, that emphasis on the superrich is misplaced: the fact that people in the 99.9th percentile of the income distribution are pulling away from those in the 90th percentile just isn't that important. A hedge fund manager in a good year may make five hundred times more than, say, a college professor, who in turn may make only five times more than a telemarketer. But in terms of what really counts in life—a chance to develop one's capacities through challenging and interesting work, and the sense of accomplishment that comes from making use of that chance—the gap between the professor and the telemarketer is far bigger and more significant. The cleavage that has opened up between America's economic elite and everybody else is therefore what I want to focus on.

That cleavage is very roughly but still usefully demarcated by the distinction between the nearly 30 percent of Americans who hold a college degree and the more than 70 percent who don't. To be sure, there are plenty of college graduates who got their diploma without accumulating much in the way of human capital and whose career prospects are less than bright (more about that in the next chapter). Meanwhile, it is still possible to learn valuable skills and do interesting, rewarding work without earning a bachelor's degree—and I'm not just talking about Bill Gates and Mark Zuckerberg. Technicians, plumbers, real estate brokers, therapists, pilots, chefs, and small business owners, among others, can earn good livings without a four-year degree.

Yet the overlap between the college-educated and the highly skilled is considerable enough to be clearly visible in the statistics. In particular, the shift from the egalitarian trends of the early postwar decades to the growing spread in incomes over the past generation is well captured by the growth of the college wage premium. Back in 1980, the average college graduate made about 30 percent more than someone with only a high school diploma; today that differential is around 70 percent. Meanwhile, the graduate degree premium has jumped from around 50 percent to more than 100 percent.[4] And not only is the upside steeper for college grads, the downside is gentler too. In 2010, as the national unemployment rate exceeded 9 percent, only 4.7 percent of workers with a bachelor's degree were out of a job. By contrast, the jobless rate was 10.3 percent for high school grads, and 14.9 percent for high school dropouts.

So what happened? Why are class divisions, now redefined along educational lines, reasserting themselves? The answer lies in two stories of polarization: one economic, one cultural.

The MIT economist David Autor has led the way in documenting and explaining a crucial shift in the evolution of the job market—not only in the United States but in advanced countries generally. In the United States, employment growth rates through the 1980s rose steadily with the skill level of the job. The highest-skill jobs grew fastest, while the lowest-skill jobs actually declined as a share of total employment. In other words, economic development took the form of a general upskilling of the occupational structure. Beginning in the 1990s, though, the graph of relative employment growth against skill level shifted from a steadily rising line to a U-shaped curve. In other words, the share of total employment rose for the highest- and lowest-skill jobs while falling for middle-skill positions. Autor refers to this new dynamic as the polarization of the labor market. And he has found that it is occurring throughout the advanced economies of the European Union as well.[5]

Why the change? Here Autor leans on his MIT colleague Frank Levy and the Harvard economist Richard Murnane, who together have identified the crucial role of the ongoing information revolution in transforming the nature of work. They argue that computing power *substitutes* for workers who perform routine, rule-based tasks and *complements* workers who engage in nonroutine problem solving and complex communication. In other words, the continuing progress of computerization is rendering middle-skill workers—those who have mastered some relatively complex but codifiable set of tasks—increasingly obsolete, while it is making the highest-skill workers more valuable than ever. Meanwhile, computerization hasn't had much effect one way or the other on a wide range of low-skill manual work—for example, personal services, construction, truck driving, and the like.[6]

Consequently, technological change is effectively hollowing out the occupational structure. The highest-skill jobs are getting a boost, middle-skill jobs are taking it on the chin, and the lowest-skill jobs are growing by default. Globalization, meanwhile, is reinforcing these trends, as first blue-collar jobs and now increasingly routine white-collar jobs as well are being shipped overseas where they can be done much more cheaply.

The upshot of these developments is that the opportunity costs of being raised in a working-class culture have risen sharply in recent decades. Previously, the existence of a large middle-skill job sector meant that class lines were blurred. In the broad middle ground, people who had developed only modest fluency with abstraction could nonetheless find work that fairly exercised their capabilities, paid relatively well, and conferred decent standing in the community. With the erosion of that middle ground, a growing gap in socioeconomic status between the highly skilled elite and everybody else has now opened up.

The rise of class-based inequality is sending a clear if unpleasant market signal: the relative value of the economic contributions made by less-skilled workers is sinking. For current workers, that is a painful and dispiriting message to receive. But for future workers, the steady and sustained broadcast of this signal has a significant potential upside. The rise in inequality is in effect saying: the working class needs to shrink and the elite needs to grow. The upper echelons of socioeconomic attainment within working-class culture are disappearing, while opportunities for those immersed in high-fluency culture continue to proliferate. The widening of the class divide has thus created a powerful economic incentive for young people from working-class backgrounds to break into the ranks of the highly skilled.

Rising inequality is often depicted as a failure of capitalism, but in fact capitalism is operating exactly as we might wish it to. It is actively encouraging more and more people to develop their capacities, to hone their skills, to put themselves in a position to find relatively interesting and challenging work. This is quite the opposite of the old Marxist vision of capitalism, in which the pursuit of profits depended on a vast, unskilled proletariat whose fate was to grow ever larger and more miserable.

Here is the problem, though: people aren't responding to economic incentives. Despite the rising returns to human capital, human capital development is slowing down or stagnating in large sections of American society. Even though dropping out of high school is now virtually a guarantee of economic failure, the high school graduation rate is lower today than it was in 1970.[7] And the college graduation rate for twenty-five- to twenty-nine-year-olds has risen only sluggishly over the past thirty years even with a big increase in the college wage premium. According to the Harvard economists Claudia Goldin and Lawrence Katz, the relative supply of college graduates rose at an average rate of only 2 percent a year between 1980 and 2005—a steep decline from the average rate of 3.8 percent a year that prevailed between 1960 and 1980.[8]

Why aren't people responding to economic incentives? Because, quite simply, culture is trumping economics. First, there is the problem of cultural inertia. Culture by its very nature is sticky: it simply *is* that which gets passed from the heads of one generation to the heads of the next. There is thus a strong tendency for children immersed since birth in working-class culture to remain in that culture throughout their adult lives.

But cultural inertia has always been with us, and it did not prevent a dramatic rise in human capital across the whole population over the course of the twentieth century—or the consequent expansion of the managerial, professional, and entrepreneurial elite over that same period. In our present circumstances we are contending with a much more serious obstacle: not just cultural inertia but cultural polarization. Over the past generation or so, elite culture has heightened its focus on fostering fluency with abstraction, while working-class culture has moved in the opposite direction. As a result, the challenges of economic polarization are much more difficult to overcome.

This cultural polarization is most obvious in the divergent trends in family structure. Over the course of the past half century, American society generally has seen a dramatic rise in single-parent families. Children born to unmarried mothers have soared from 10 percent of the total in 1969 to an astonishing 41 percent in 2008. Meanwhile, the share of children living with two married parents has fallen from 77 percent in 1980 to 65 percent in 2011.[9]

It is well known that these aggregate figures mask large disparities along racial lines. Thus, as of 2008, 29 percent of white, non-Hispanic children were born to single mothers, compared to 53 percent of Hispanic children and 72 percent of black children. And in 2011, 75 percent of white, non-Hispanic children were living with two married parents, while the same could be said for 60 percent of Hispanic children and only 33 percent of black children. What is less well known is that these racial cleavages are largely explained by a similar divide along class lines. As of 2011, 87 percent of children who have a parent with a bachelor's or higher degree were living with two married parents. The corresponding figures for high school grads and high school dropouts were 53 and 47 percent, respectively.

A major contributor to the growing class differences in family structure is the emergence in recent decades of a "divorce divide" along educational lines. Divorce rates have traditionally been lower for college-educated couples than for the rest of the population, but marriage breakup rates for everybody soared during the 1960s and 1970s. For women whose first marriage occurred between 1970 and 1974, the share whose marriage failed within ten years stood at 24.3 percent for those with a college degree or better and 33.7 percent for the rest. But since the 1970s, divorce rates among the highly educated have fallen significantly; among non–college grads, by contrast, they have stayed high. Specifically, only 16.7 percent of women with at least a college degree experienced a marital dissolution within ten years of a first marriage between 1990 and 1994—a 31 percent drop from twenty years earlier. For other women, though, the marriage breakup rate in the latter period was now 35.7 percent—6 percent higher than twenty years earlier.[10]

Interestingly, the divergence in divorce rates is matched—and at least partially explained—by a parallel divergence in attitudes about divorce. Back in the 1970s, responses to the question "Should divorces be easier or harder to obtain?" were quite similar across educational lines, with college-educated women slightly more liberal in their attitudes than others. But by 2000–2002, college-educated women had shifted strongly in favor of making divorce less available; women with a high school diploma or some college moved slightly in the same direction, while high school dropouts now were much more likely to favor easy divorce.[11]

The collapse of the traditional nuclear family structure among the less educated has made for a much less favorable environment for human capital formation. A large number of studies have documented that children of traditional nuclear families have better educational outcomes—and thus better career opportunities—than children of single-parent or "blended" families (i.e., with stepparents or half siblings). It's true, of course, that some of this correlation may be due to other, underlying factors. For example, parents with good social skills and impulse control may be more likely both to hold their marriages together and to impart these useful traits to their children (whether through their genes or their parenting). Along these lines, it is worth noting that parental absence due to death is associated with a much lesser adverse impact on educational outcomes than is absence due to divorce.

Nevertheless, given how exotic the skills of fluency with abstraction are, and thus how much time they take to develop and master, it is to be expected that families without the resources (in the case of single parents) or motivation (in the case of some stepparents) to dedicate large amounts of time to intensive child rearing will be at a real disadvantage. Accordingly, there is little reason to doubt that changes in family structure are part and parcel of a larger process of cultural polarization.

Cultural polarization is being exacerbated by changing patterns of child rearing. A number of recent studies have revealed the surprising finding that, despite how harried we all feel, parents have actually been spending more time with their kids over the course of recent decades (maybe that's why we feel so harried!). A 2007 study, for example, found that married women devoted an average of 12.9 hours a week to child care in 2000, up from 10.6 hours back in 1965. Married men, meanwhile, more than doubled the time they spent taking care of their children over the same period—from 2.6 hours to 6.5 hours per week.[12] Although single mothers have also upped the hours they spend on child care, the gap in child care time between single-parent and nuclear families has been growing. And since intact nuclear families are now disproportionately more common among the college-educated, that means that the general trend toward more intensive parenting is widening the class divide.

And more recent research by the husband-and-wife economists Garey and Valerie Ramey shows that, not surprisingly, the increased commitment to child care is especially pronounced among well-educated parents. Prior to 1995, college-educated moms averaged about 12 hours a week with their kids, compared to about 11 hours for less-educated moms; by 2007, though, the figure for less-educated moms had risen to 15.9 hours while that for college-educated moms had soared all the way to 21.2 hours. Similar trends were observed for fathers: the time that college-educated dads spent with their kids rose from around 5 hours a week to 10 hours, while for less-educated dads the increase was from around 4 hours to around 8 hours.[13]

The increase in time spent on child care is part of a larger shift in parenting style that now distinguishes elite culture from the rest of American society. As discussed earlier, the sociologist Annette Lareau has identified a clear, class-based difference in parenting styles. Among the poor and working-class families she observed and studied, the focus of parenting was on what she calls "the accomplishment of natural growth." In these families, "parents viewed children's development as unfolding spontaneously, as long as they were provided with comfort, food, shelter, and other basic support." By contrast, for middle-class families with college-educated parents, the aim is "concerted cultivation." "In these families," Lareau writes, "parents actively fostered and assessed their children's talents, opinions, and skills. They scheduled their children for activities. They reasoned with them. . . . *They made a deliberate and sustained effort to stimulate children's development and to cultivate their cognitive and social skills.*"[14]

The emergence of "concerted cultivation" parenting, at least at its current level of intensity, is of relatively recent vintage—as witness the spate of references to "superkids," "organization kids," "overparenting," and "helicopter parents" over the past couple of decades. In earlier decades, parents across class lines stuck pretty closely to the more laissez-faire parenting style that Lareau calls "the accomplishment of natural growth." The big spike in time spent on child care by college-educated parents is evidence of the adoption of a different approach—one in which parents focus relentlessly on ensuring that their children are fluent in the abstract art of modern living.

When it comes to providing their children with an environment that is either favorable or hostile to human capital formation, the elite and everybody else have thus been moving in opposite directions over the past generation. Among families with college-educated parents, marriages have been growing more stable, parents have dramatically increased the time they spend with their kids, and they are spending that time in a dedicated effort to foster the intellectual, social, and personal skills needed to thrive in an ever more complicated world. In the rest of the country, by contrast, the percentage of children born to single mothers has skyrocketed, divorce rates remain high, and parents continue to practice the old, laissez-faire style of parenting. Thus, at precisely the same time changes in the workplace have brought about economic polarization, changes in the home have ushered in an era of cultural polarization.

It seems reasonably clear that computerization and globalization are the main culprits behind economic polarization. But what has been driving the simultaneous divergence in child-rearing environments? No clear answer has emerged from social science, but my own view is that the phenomenon is largely due to other, broader cultural changes that swept through American society in the 1960s and 1970s. As I've written about in a previous book, the advent of mass affluence in the decades after World War II provoked a fundamental reorientation in norms, beliefs, and values—away from the traditional, scarcity-constrained ethos of self-denial in favor of a new, abundance-enabled ethos of self-realization.[15] The political scientist Ronald Inglehart, whose pioneering work has documented the global diffusion of this cultural shift, refers to it as the move from "survival" to "self-expression" values.[16]

As part of this shift, absolutist conceptions of morality have given way to more relativistic, context-dependent conceptions. And, in particular, enforcement of moral norms through shaming and ostracizing has faltered in the face of a growing reticence about seeming overly judgmental and a preference instead for leaving matters to each individual's own conscience. To lay my own cards on the table, I embrace this less censorious, more individualistic approach to moral judgment and regard it as more enlightened than what it replaced, and I suspect most of the people who reads books like this one do too. Yet all of us should face up to the fact that this moral revolution, like most revolutions, has had some baleful if unintended consequences.

Specifically, the effects of greater social tolerance have played out very differently on either side of the class divide. For members of the elite, the cultural shift has proven overwhelmingly liberating. Flush with human capital, in particular the skills I call fluency with personal abstraction, they are happily rid of hectoring busybodies and narrow-minded scolds. Highly skilled in subjugating short-term desires to long-term goals, they have thrived by relying on their own consciences, thank you very much. But members of the working class, less steeped in modern complexity and thus less facile with abstraction in all its dimensions, are consequently less adept at deferring gratification. For them, the loss of external props to self-discipline has meant that short-sighted, destructive behavior—of particular concern here, having children outside marriage and failing to make marriages work—is considerably less constrained than it was for earlier generations. And thus, sadly, more prevalent.

Charles Murray, who looked to genes to explain class differences in *The Bell Curve*, has now focused on the cultural underpinnings of class-based inequality in his provocative new book *Coming Apart*. The book is full of in-depth descriptions of the cultural polarization I have just described. When it comes to explaining what has happened, though, Murray offers little more than plaintive moralizing. He sees the cultural changes that have occurred since the 1960s as, quite simply, a decline in virtue—most directly on the part of the working class, but indirectly as well among members of the elite who, while thriving on their own, have abdicated moral leadership by failing to "preach what they practice."[17]

I'm afraid this approach doesn't get us anywhere. The absolutist conceptions of morality that once kept the working class (and everybody else, too) on the straight and narrow were a cultural adaptation to material scarcity. As Inglehart has documented exhaustively, when scarcity abates, these absolutist conceptions lose their hold on people's hearts and minds—not just in the United States but around the world. We may wish it were otherwise, but wishing won't change things. There is simply no prospect for a return to the more authoritarian morality of yesteryear.

But the fact that the American elite is thriving today shows that virtue—in terms of a strong work ethic, commitment to family life, and active inculcation of useful skills in the next generation—can survive the demise of old-style morality. Practicing this virtue, however, relies on a well-developed capacity for abstraction—namely, the ability to imagine a hypothetical future self vividly enough to motivate impulse control in the here and now. Members of the working class don't need judgmental sermonizing from those higher on the socioeconomic scale. What they need are the skills to practice virtue in the same way the elite now does—skills in personal abstraction that are capable of being learned by the vast majority of the population.

The sharpening of class differences in recent decades is being driven by two different forms of polarization, each of which is a consequence of economic development. In the labor market, the progress of globalization and the information revolution is thinning out the middle-skill elements of the occupational structure. In the cultural sphere, the material security of mass affluence has encouraged the rise of a more permissive attitude toward sex and family life. Both of these trends have worked to widen the divide between people who are fluent with abstraction and those who aren't.

Here then is the challenge that confronts us: to overcome the widening disparities caused by economic polarization, we need to devise policies that will work to halt and reverse cultural polarization. The rise of human capitalism has brought tremendous benefits—not just the material abundance we enjoy as consumers but also the development of our innate capacities that we then employ as producers. Unfortunately, in recent decades, just as the incentives for the further development of those capacities have sharpened considerably, cultural obstacles have hindered many people from responding to those incentives.

The silver lining of this state of affairs is that, over the past generation, the ongoing development of human capitalism has built up a huge backlog of untapped potential gains. The demand for human capital has continued to grow apace even as the supply has stalled. As a result, if policies more favorable to spreading the culture of high abstraction can be implemented, ample opportunities for upward mobility will be available. There is plenty of room at the top; we just need to clear the route to the summit.

Seven
Reforming Human Capitalism

The emergence of human capitalism is a stupendously beneficial achievement that has brought enormous human progress. The rise of social complexity has catalyzed the development of cognitive capabilities on an unprecedented scale. Educational attainment has soared, and the division of labor has shifted from one deeply dependent on brute manual labor to one ever more heavily reliant on the ever more elaborate honing of talents and skills.

And yet . . . . At the same time there is a big problem: this progress has been extremely uneven. And these days, alas, this problem is much more salient than all the benefits, as concerns about mass unemployment, stagnating incomes, and widening inequality cast deep shadows on both individuals' prospects and the nation's. Over the past generation, the promise of human capitalism has not been realized: although an elite upper third or so continues to take advantage of its proliferating opportunities, for everybody else the connection between increasing complexity and rising skill levels has frayed or even snapped. Educational attainment has stalled, and the lowest-skill jobs are increasing, not decreasing, their share of total employment.

In the previous chapter I explained why I think this is happening. Here's the bottom line: economic development and cultural development have gotten out of sync with each other. Economic growth is continuing to add to social complexity, and as a result the demand for people with high human capital—that is, people who are fluent with abstraction—keeps going up and up. Yet for most Americans, cultural change has been moving in the opposite direction. Most American kids are now raised in an environment that is arguably less favorable for developing human capital than that in which their parents were raised.

This conflict between economics and culture poses a serious threat to the future vitality of human capitalism. First, of course, there is the threat of squandered potential: the growing demand for more highly skilled workers—which makes possible the growing supply of interesting, challenging jobs—is going unfulfilled. More ominous, there is the threat that widening disparities between the elite and everybody else will prompt a political backlash against the whole system. That backlash could well take the form of policy changes that undermine future economic growth—with a resulting diminution in the possibilities for further social progress. Potential unrealized is bad enough, but potential eliminated altogether is even worse.

To redeem the promise of human capitalism, it is necessary to restore the connection between rising complexity and rising human capital across the socioeconomic spectrum. For that to happen, we need public policies that encourage healthy cultural change. Policies to reshape the environment in which most Americans are born and raised so that it promotes rather than hinders their development of the intellectual, social, and personal skills needed to cope with social complexity. And policies to remove barriers that currently discourage people from making use of the capabilities they already possess and then building on them.

This is a huge and difficult undertaking, to be sure. Culture, by its very nature, is extremely sticky: propagating itself from one generation to the next is quite simply what a culture *does*, and attempts to intervene in and redirect that process must overcome powerful forces of inertia. Any successes in this endeavor will always be gradual and dispersed along countless different margins; there is no one "silver bullet" that will magically change people's beliefs, values, and habits in the desired direction.

Yet the fact is that culture changes all the time, and public policy can have a powerful influence on the long-term direction of that change. It is good to recall the words of Daniel Patrick Moynihan, the public intellectual turned U.S. senator. "The central conservative truth," Moynihan wrote, "is that it is culture, not politics, that determines the success of a society." But then, he added, "The central liberal truth is that politics can change a culture and save it from itself."[1]

But how exactly do we go about effecting the changes that are needed? What follows in this concluding chapter is a proposed policy agenda for reforming human capitalism. This agenda makes no pretense of being comprehensive. Many other worthy ideas could be added. The point here is merely to sketch some of the diverse angles from which the central problem of human capitalism can be constructively addressed. And that central problem is: how do we encourage wider exposure to and participation in the complex tasks of modern life? People who are immersed in social complexity and constantly called on to engage in complex tasks will naturally develop a greater facility with abstraction than people who are less exposed and less challenged. And, in turn, people with more human capital will be much likelier to find themselves immersed in complexity and called on to perform complex tasks. Adding momentum to this virtuous circle at various points along the curve is the common aim that unites what at first may seem a mere grab bag of proposals into a coherent reform project.

■ Maintain Economic Growth by Encouraging Entrepreneurship

The starting point of any program for more broad-based development of human capital must be to ensure that economic growth remains as robust as possible. In light of growing inequality, many people have come to question the utility of continued growth: what does it matter if the pie keeps expanding when a select few gobble up most of the gains? Yet if growth by itself isn't sufficient, it's certainly a necessary precondition for the kind of progress we are seeking.

The reason is the inextricable connection between modern economic growth and rising social complexity. As has been known since Robert Solow did his Nobel Prize–winning work, the vast majority of growth in advanced countries comes not from the mere expansion of existing activities (i.e., increased inputs of capital and labor) but from innovation—new ideas, new products, and new production techniques.[2] And innovation necessarily adds to the complexity of the social order: first, by expanding the total amount of knowledge and know-how distributed throughout the system, and second, by increasing specialization in the division of labor.

With greater complexity come greater opportunities to perform complex tasks—and develop complex skills. As discussed earlier, growth leads to what can be called the "cephalization" of economic life: just as animals that engage in more complex behaviors have higher brain-to-body ratios, so a richer, more complex economy requires relatively greater brainpower to operate. In short, the natural consequence of further growth is increased demand for human capital. And since the main aim of reform here is to increase the supply of human capital, ensuring that there is a demand for the extra increment supplied is the first order of business.

Research performed and supported by the Kauffman Foundation makes clear that the key to maintaining vibrant growth is a favorable policy environment for entrepreneurs who start and build innovative new businesses. For example, the data show that firms exiting the market are generally less productive than existing firms, which in turn are less productive than surviving new firms.[3] Thus, the ongoing churn of what Joseph Schumpeter called "creative destruction"—and, in particular, the entry of new firms—is essential to introducing and diffusing valuable new ideas into and throughout the economy.

The issue isn't really "big" versus "small" government. Economic dynamism can coexist with relatively high levels of social spending and a strong regulatory apparatus, and the absence of those manifestations of "big government" is no guarantee of a vibrant and prosperous economy. What is needed, rather, is the combination of economic freedom and proper incentives. By economic freedom I mean the freedom of competitive market forces to operate without interference—for example, the freedom of new firms to enter the marketplace and struggling ones to close down, the freedom of businesses to hire and fire workers, the freedom of prices to move in response to supply and demand, and the freedom from government interventions in the form of "picking winners." Meanwhile, it is vitally important that tax and regulatory policies, whatever their other objectives, are structured so as to preserve strong incentives to compete and innovate—and avoid perverse incentives to engage in unproductive (i.e., "rent-seeking") activity.[4]

■ **Reform K–12 Education by Unleashing Competition**

Nowhere is an invigorating dose of entrepreneurship more desperately needed than in primary and secondary education. Schools are the social institutions most directly responsible for human capital formation, so they are the obvious first target for reform in any effort to boost human capital levels. And the pressing need for reform is beyond serious dispute. Since 1970, real (i.e., inflation-adjusted) spending per pupil in public primary and secondary schools has more than doubled, while test scores have remained more or less flat. Any system in which a doubling of inputs leads to no significant increase in output is a broken system. Fundamental, structural change is therefore needed.

And the basic structural flaw in the U.S. school system today is the absence of competition. Some 90 percent of K–12 pupils attend government-run public schools, and the vast majority of them attend schools to which they have been assigned. Most schools thus have captive customers—and correspondingly reduced incentives to serve their customers well. A measure of competition still exists in the form of residential choice, but having to buy an expensive home in order to get your kids into a good school is hardly a direct or effective way to pressure schools to improve. Meanwhile, the modest effects of even this kind of competition have been attenuated over time. After all, much of what happens in individual schools is controlled at the school district level. Yet between 1930 and 1970, the number of school districts in the United States plummeted from around 120,000 to around 16,000, and since then the number has continued to drift downward.[5] At the same time, more and more decision-making power over what takes place in the classroom has migrated from the local level up to state and federal education bureaucracies.

Any reforms that move decision-making authority and accountability downward are steps in the right direction. Teacher certification rules need to be loosened so that schools of education no longer monopolize the training of teachers. Principals and teachers need greater power over deciding what goes on in the classroom. Parents need more freedom in choosing where to send their kids to school. And schools need to be able to grow or shrink based on those parental choices. Reforms associated with the "school choice" movement—private school vouchers and tax credits, charter schools, and home schooling—obviously figure prominently in this agenda. But given that most kids attend traditional public schools and will probably continue to do so for the foreseeable future, the agenda needs to encompass changing how traditional public schools are managed as well as creating alternatives to them. Collective bargaining agreements should be overhauled to create greater flexibility in hiring, firing, promoting, and paying teachers. "Weighted student funding"—in which parents are allowed to choose which public schools their kids attend and schools' budgets then reflect those choices—has been adopted with promising results in a number of large urban school districts and deserves to be tried more broadly. Other measures to decentralize the operation of school districts, or to break them up into smaller districts, should be encouraged as well.

It must be noted that research to date shows mixed results for school choice initiatives. The usual metric is standardized test results, but ensuring proper comparisons is methodologically tricky since better scores by voucher or charter school students may simply reflect preexisting differences between those kids (and their presumably more motivated parents) and the rest of their peers. In any event, some studies show significant academic gains for children in school choice programs while others do not.

Here's what we can say with confidence. First of all, school choice by itself is no panacea. As the education researcher Frederick Hess points out, Soviet citizens had plenty of retail "choice"—lots of different stores with not much on their shelves to pick from.[6] What matters isn't choice alone—it's choice in the context of functioning, well-structured, competitive markets. So the design of school choice programs is crucially important. Furthermore, although even well-designed programs can't guarantee great results, they can dramatically improve the incentives under which schools operate—and open a path for educational entrepreneurs to innovate and for successful innovations to be more widely adopted.

And here's the really good news: recent evidence shows that innovative, high-quality schools can have a significant impact on closing the culture gap and reducing class-based differences in scholastic achievement and life prospects. A number of studies of well-run charter schools show sizable academic gains for poor and minority students. These studies ensure "apples-to-apples" comparisons by looking at schools that use lotteries to determine which applicants to accept; the academic performance of the accepted students is then compared to that of lottery losers. Reviewing the evidence, Harvard economist Roland Fryer concludes, "providing high-quality schools to children who live in low-quality environments can significantly increase their achievement."[7]

These results are highly encouraging, but caution is still in order. After all, the history of education reform is littered with promising early results that didn't pan out. In particular, it remains an open question whether the results of these high-quality charter schools are scalable. It is one thing for a small number of schools run by visionary administrators and highly dedicated teachers to achieve great things. But can similar results be achieved on a mass scale by presumably less extraordinary professionals? Only then will real, meaningful social change occur.

■ **Compensate for Disadvantaged Environments through Early Childhood Interventions**

The task confronting schools charged with closing the culture gap is such a daunting one in large part because schooling starts so relatively late in the game. Training our minds to adapt to the highly exotic conditions of modern social complexity is an arduous process best begun as early as possible. In the families of the socioeconomic elite, the process commences at birth, so that by the time less advantaged kids start school they are already far behind. In this regard, recall the finding of child psychologists Hart and Risley that, by the age of three, there is already a thirty-million-word gap in the verbal stimulation received by poor kids compared to those in upper-middle-class families.

So it seems eminently logical that any agenda to spur more broad-based human capital development should include efforts aimed at very young children. What is needed are interventions that expose kids from disadvantaged backgrounds to the culture of cognitive complexity. The exposure needs to be of sufficient intensity and duration to change their life trajectories—to begin the virtuous circle of facing complex challenges, mastering them, and finding in that sense of mastery the motivation to take on further challenges.

Unfortunately, the actual track record of programs along these lines has been disappointing. Best-known, the Head Start program begun during the War on Poverty in the 1960s has succeeded in boosting kids' scholastic readiness while they are in the program. The gains, however, don't last: within a couple years, there is no discernible difference between kids who went through Head Start and everybody else.[8]

Meanwhile, Roland Fryer has recently investigated the community-based interventions of the Harlem Children's Zone, a well-known effort to serve disadvantaged kids and their families in a ninety-seven-block area of New York City. The HCZ features a variety of enrichment and support programs as well as high-quality charter schools for elementary and middle-school students. The community programs are available only to residents of the area, while the schools are open to outsiders as well. If the community programs were making a difference, charter school students who live inside the zone should have a leg up on other kids. Yet Fryer found no difference in achievement gains between the two sets of kids. Indeed, he found no correlation between participation in HCZ programs and academic achievement at all.[9]

Despite these discouraging results, the promise of early childhood interventions should not be dismissed. Of particular interest is the research of James Heckman, a Nobel Prize–winning economist at the University of Chicago and one of the world's foremost experts on human capital formation. Heckman argues vehemently in favor of the effectiveness of such interventions, relying on evidence from a handful of programs that have done long-term follow-up studies of their participants—including the Perry Preschool experiment in Ypsilanti, Michigan, which ran from 1962 to 1967; the Abecedarian project in Chapel Hill, North Carolina, which ran from 1972 to 1977; and the Child Parent Centers in Chicago, which began in 1967 and continue in operation today.

Heckman's claims for these programs are modest but nonetheless significant. He does not argue that they were able to close the achievement gap or transform children from the underclass into upper-middle-class adults. He does contend, however, that the programs were cost-effective: that the benefits in terms of reduced crime and welfare dependency in adulthood more than compensated for the costs. In particular, his in-depth study of the Perry Preschool finds that this particular program had a return on investment in the range of 7 to 10 percent per year—not eye-popping, but still better than the long-term average returns on investing in stocks.[10] So the right interventions at the right ages may not work miracles, but they can change life trajectories enough to make a real difference.

The lack of any miracle cures from early childhood interventions demonstrates the formidable power of the cultural inertia that they seek to overcome. Despite the difficulties, though, there are solid grounds for continuing to push forward with further experiments. Early childhood is where the culture gap begins and grows, so it is hard to argue against trying to address the problem at its root. Meanwhile, as Heckman has documented, some kinds of programs have achieved lasting benefits for the kids who go through them—and for the rest of society as well. The agenda for reforming human capitalism must therefore include ongoing initiatives to learn from past successes and failures and give disadvantaged kids access to the enriched and stimulating environment that is the launching pad for socioeconomic achievement.

It is premature, however, to move ahead with any new large-scale initiatives at the federal or even state level. In particular, proponents of universal pre-K are fond of citing Heckman's research as supporting their case, but Heckman himself has made clear that the evidence doesn't support the utility of early childhood intervention except in the case of kids from disadvantaged backgrounds.[11] Other kids already receive at home the kind of attention and stimulation that intervention programs offer, and thus the institution of universal pre-K would entail vastly greater costs than targeted programs without offering any significant additional gains in school readiness. With regard to targeted programs, what is needed right now is more experimentation at the small scale to see what approaches work best. After all, we already have a federal early childhood program, Head Start, and it doesn't work very well. Before we overhaul it or expand it, we need a much clearer sense of why its results have been so disappointing.

■ Combat Social Exclusion of Low-Skilled Adults

School reform and early childhood interventions aim to broaden the future ranks of Americans who are fluent with abstraction and capable of thriving in the midst of social complexity. Of course, those efforts will never be universally successful, and in any event the majority of adult Americans today lack high human capital. How can a human capitalism reform agenda brighten their prospects?

I believe that the most morally urgent priority when it comes to helping less-skilled adults is essentially defensive: to reduce the downside risks of falling altogether out of meaningful, productive participation in the joint social enterprise. Particular attention should be paid to policies that encourage work and reverse the alarming rise of mass incarceration.

Once upon a time, the terms *working class* and *leisure class* were rooted in economic reality. In other words, the poor worked much longer hours than did the rich, who often lived off their wealth and didn't have to work at all. Now, however, the situation is reversed. In the United States today, working-age adults in the top quintile of the income distribution work about twice as many hours a year as their counterparts in the bottom quintile. The reason for this disparity is that many low-skilled people work only irregularly if at all. Consider the yawning gap in labor-force participation along educational lines: as of 2005, 78 percent of college graduates twenty-five years or older were in the active workforce, compared to only 46 percent of high school dropouts.

Rampant joblessness among the less skilled is a terrible social blight. It is a major cause not only of poverty but of crime, substance abuse, alienation, and despair as well—not just for the adults who are marginalized by their failure to contribute to the economy, but also for the children raised in this deprived environment and thereby condemned to recreate it in their adulthood.

Accordingly, policies are needed that actively encourage work among the less skilled. Human capital, however modest, is better employed than wasted, and making use of what you have is the only path to acquiring more—not just for yourself but for your kids as well. We have already seen progress in developing prowork social policies: the welfare reforms of 1996 instituted work requirements, and the Earned Income Tax Credit conditions benefits on paid employment. Another interesting proposal along similar lines comes from the Nobel Prize–winning economist Edmund Phelps, who has proposed a new system of subsidies to employers who hire low-wage workers.[12] As opposed to transfer payments and in-kind services that undermine the incentive to work, Phelps's plan would cut in the opposite direction by making employment opportunities for the less skilled both more plentiful and more attractive.

Another way to raise labor-force participation would be by reforming Social Security Disability Insurance. Even as the health of older working-age Americans has been generally improving, relaxed eligibility criteria have spurred rapid growth in the SSDI rolls over the past couple of decades. The percentage of adults receiving benefits under the program doubled from 2.3 percent to 4.6 percent between 1989 and 2009. Costs over the same period have soared, with cash payments tripling (in inflation-adjusted terms) to $121 billion annually and Medicare costs for beneficiaries climbing from $18 billion to $69 billion. Much of the growth has come from a flood of less skilled workers into the program.

As currently designed, SSDI actively discourages work by conditioning benefits on joblessness. Many workers with health issues could continue in their jobs with some rehabilitation or reasonable accommodation in the workplace, but under the present system nobody has any incentive to incur the expenses that can keep people employed. One reform possibility would be to institute experience rating for employers' contributions to the SSDI payroll tax. Such a move would create incentives for firms to provide workplace accommodations for disabled workers when practicable rather than simply laying them off. Alternatively, the currently flat payroll tax rate could be changed to a system with two brackets: a lower rate for employers who offer private short-term disability insurance to their workers, and a higher rate for those who don't.[13]

An even starker and more destructive form of social exclusion than joblessness is imprisonment. Although the problem has started to receive increased attention in recent years, the calamitous spike in the nation's prison population since the 1970s remains woefully underreported. For decades, the proportion of Americans locked up in jail and prison held steady at around 100 per 100,000 people. Today the figure stands at an astonishing 700 per 100,000—the highest incarceration rate in the world, higher than autocratic regimes like Russia and China, and many times higher than the rate in other advanced democracies.

Unsurprisingly, the burden falls especially heavily on the poor and minorities. African Americans, who make up only 13 percent of the nation's overall population, constitute fully half the nation's inmates. The incarceration rate for black men is some seven-and-a-half times that of whites. Here's the depressing bottom line: one out of three African American men can expect to spend some time behind bars during his lifetime.[14]

Of course the rise of mass imprisonment occurred in delayed response to the dramatic increase in crime rates that began in the 1960s. And keeping dangerous felons locked up and off the streets has certainly been an important factor in the sharp fall in crime since the mid-1990s. Yet the prison population has continued to balloon even with the fall in crime rates, and experts estimate that changes in incarceration policy account for only 10 to 35 percent of the decline.[15] Meanwhile, even with some 2.3

million people behind bars, those crime rates are still significantly higher than they were when the crime wave of the 1960s commenced.

There has to be a better way. The lock-'em-up strategy for dealing with crime long ago hit the wall of diminishing returns. And the human toll of the ensuing overkill has been tremendous—not only for the people inside the system but also for their families and wider communities. The idea of prison as rehabilitation has lost any connection with reality: time in prison undermines future prospects for both work and marriage, disrupts the lives of children, and ultimately breeds more crime with sky-high recidivism rates.

If we are serious about reducing prison populations while avoiding increased danger to law-abiding citizens, a critical reexamination of the nation's drug laws should be a top priority. Some four hundred thousand people are currently in state or federal prison for drug-related offenses—more than 15 percent of all inmates.[16] And as with alcohol prohibition before it, drug prohibition breeds crime by creating lucrative black markets for distributors and dealers to profit from. A fundamental rethink of drug policy is in order: drug abuse needs to be treated as a public health issue, not a crime issue, and resources should be devoted to public education and treatment rather than law enforcement.

More broadly, a new approach to managing probation and parole violations holds out hope for reducing both crime and punishment simultaneously. The basic idea is to substitute predictable, immediate, and relatively mild punishment for the uncertain, long-delayed, and much harsher penalties that are typically doled out. The model here is a program in Hawaii called HOPE, in which probationers who missed or flunked a drug test were brought into court within forty-eight hours and sent immediately to jail for a few days. The program began with chronic violators and immediately showed results: the prospect of swift, sure, relatively light punishment led to a big drop in violations. With the workload more manageable, the program was then able to expand to include more probationers. And the results of a randomized controlled trial showed that offenders in the program had fewer drug problems and spent much less time locked up. HOPE now includes about one-sixth of all felony probationers in Hawaii, and strikingly this expansion of a zero-tolerance policy has been accomplished without having to add any new judges, clerks, or courtrooms (new drug testers and additional treatment services were added).

Mark Kleiman, a professor of public policy at UCLA and a leading expert on crime and drug policy, believes that the HOPE model can be expanded to revolutionize the criminal justice system.[17] If probationers and parolees were given an anklet with a GPS receiver and a transmitter, the zero-tolerance policy used for drug tests could be applied to other terms and conditions like curfews, restraining orders, and requirements to go to work on time. "With such a system in place, judges would have a real alternative to incarceration," Kleiman writes. "If the 'outpatient prison' could do for recidivism among parolees what HOPE did for new crimes by probationers, five years from now we could have many fewer people in prison than we do today, and half as much crime."[18]

▪ Improve Higher Education
by Limiting Tuition Subsidies

America's higher education system has long enjoyed a strong reputation—in stark contrast to the withering criticism regularly lobbed at K–12 schooling. And for some very good reasons: the rich diversity of its institutions, for one thing, and of course the world-class scholarship of the country's leading research universities. Students from around the world seek to study here, and U.S. colleges are now branching out with foreign campuses.[19]

But notwithstanding real strengths, the problems with American postsecondary education are serious and mounting. The quality of instruction appears to be falling, costs are definitely skyrocketing, and a steep rise in the dropout rate means a big influx of new students into the system is not translating into a corresponding increase in new grads.

In a recent landmark study titled *Academically Adrift*, the sociologists Richard Arum and Josipa Roksa come to the depressing conclusion that "American higher education is characterized by limited or no learning for a large proportion of students."[20] Specifically, they tested a representative sample of more than 2,300 undergraduates using the Collegiate Learning Assessment, a standardized test designed to measure analytical reasoning, critical thinking, and communication skills. If the value of a college education really lies less in the specific subjects studied than in "learning how to think," that value should show up as rising scores on the CLA. Yet Arum and Roksa found that 45 percent of students showed no significant gains in their scores after two years in college. On average students improved their scores by only 0.18 standard deviation; in other words, after two years, a sophomore who had scored in the fiftieth percentile at the beginning of her freshman year would have scored in the fifty-seventh percentile of an incoming freshman class.[21]

It is possible to take issue with Arum and Roksa's methodology,[22] but other findings point in the same direction. Back in 1961, full-time college students reported studying twenty-five hours a week on average; by 2003, average studying time had fallen by almost half, down to thirteen hours a week. And half of students today don't take any courses that require more than twenty pages of writing over the course of a full semester.[23] Given what we know about the essential role of practice in developing expertise, the conclusion that college students are learning less than they used to seems unavoidable.

How can the wage premium for college grads have risen so steeply even as academic standards have fallen? Part of the answer boils down to a combination of supply and demand and signaling. The demand for workers with high human capital has risen ahead of the new supply, and a college degree remains the leading signal that employers use to determine that workers have the requisite skills. In other words, even if people don't learn much useful in college, the people who earn college degrees tend on average to be smarter and more conscientious than nongrads. The quality of that signal may have degraded as the skill level of the marginal grad has fallen, but it's still better than anything else employers have to go on.

There's more to the story, though, and it's not good news for those marginal college grads. Yes, the *average* college graduate enjoys a hefty wage premium, but averages can be deceiving. These days, approximately half of college grads with humanities degrees are working in jobs that don't require a college degree—and earning decidedly less than premium wages. The average grad in one of those jobs earns only $16,000, compared to an average salary of $27,000 for grads with jobs that require a degree.[24]

If job prospects are less than bright for the marginal college *grad*, the outlook is even less promising for the marginal college *attendee*. In response to the spike in the college wage premium, the number of people attending college has risen sharply in recent years. In 1980, 30 percent of new high school grads were enrolled in a four-year institution by the fall of that year; by 2009 that figure had risen to 42 percent.[25] Meanwhile, though, rates of college completion have fallen, so that the dropout rate is now around 40 percent. And the economic rewards of, say, two years of college are far less than half those of completing a degree.[26]

Stacked against the modest benefits of going to college for many marginal students are the skyrocketing costs of tuition and student loan debt. Over the past thirty years, the inflation-adjusted cost of attending college has risen by more than 340 percent—far outpacing the much better known escalation of health care costs.[27] And consequently, student loans now top $100 billion a year—up 56 percent on an inflation-adjusted, per-student basis. About two-thirds of college grads leave school today with debt, and the average amount outstanding has now risen to $25,000.[28]

Driving college's deteriorating value proposition are subsidies in the form of government-provided grants and student loans. Colleges, eager for more and more federally guaranteed revenue, have been lowering standards to boost the ranks of their student bodies. And the downward spiral in educational quality has been matched by an upward spiral of costs and subsidies—subsidies allow colleges to hike their tuition and fees, which in turn creates a political demand for more lavish subsidies, and so it goes.[29]

Although it seems counterintuitive, the best way to ensure accessible, affordable, and effective higher education over the long run is to limit the very subsidies that now help so many people in the short run. The ultimate effect of the current student loan program is to prop up institutions that offer declining quality at rising costs—and that's not good for students or taxpayers. Much stiffer conditions on access to student loans should be imposed to ensure that higher education providers don't saddle their students with debt while failing to teach them marketable skills. Currently there are rules in place that can revoke institutions' eligibility for federal subsidies if students' default rates or debt-to-income ratios climb too high, but the standards are far too lax and do not apply to enough institutions and programs.

Admittedly, retrenchment on access to subsidized loans would cause short-term pain. Fewer student loans would be issued and, in the short term at least, fewer people may end up going to college. But over time, popping the higher education "bubble" would clear the way for new, entrepreneurial higher education providers that use information technology and third-party certification to offer real value for students at a fraction of the present cost. Already, innovative new institutions like the University of the People, Western Governors University, and StraighterLine are experimenting along these lines, and more are sure to follow.

One promising reform proposal is to shift some of the current funding for student loans away from traditional institutions and toward these new-style providers regardless of whether they meet current accreditation standards—with tight limits on prices that can be charged to ensure that this new, emerging sector doesn't get sucked into the subsidy-fueled tuition spiral.[30]

America's research universities and liberal arts colleges are a great national asset, and they will continue to serve a vital function for the foreseeable future. But the higher education system overall is in serious need of a shakeup—and, as usual, the best way to shake things up is to clear the way for entrepreneurs with new ideas and new ways of doing things. What is needed is a vibrant, diverse marketplace for postsecondary instruction so that people of all ages and from widely different backgrounds can continue to develop their skills on a lifelong basis.

■ **Remove Regulatory Barriers
to Entrepreneurship and Upward Mobility**

Reforming education from early preschool through higher education promises to broaden opportunities through promoting broader human capital development—in particular, by upgrading people's fluency with intellectual abstraction. At the same time, though, we have to recognize that the capacity to develop that fluency is not evenly distributed. So what are the prospects for that sizable chunk of the population who, whatever their other gifts, just never perform that well in the classroom? Is there some alternative path to upward mobility—and, if there is, how can it be made more accessible and traversable?

If we look ahead and attempt to spy where things are heading, there are good reasons for believing that the economic polarization of recent decades can give way to a future in which excelling at schoolwork is relatively less important to future socioeconomic success. Major regulatory reforms will be needed, however, to clear the way for this more inclusive future to unfold.

Consider this deep-seated and long-running trend: the richer we get, the more we shift our consumption away from acquiring yet more stuff in favor of enjoying good experiences. Classic materialistic expenditures on food for home consumption, clothing, housing, and household operation (furniture, utilities, etc.) accounted for 64 percent of personal consumer spending in 1950 but had fallen to 40 percent by 2000. By contrast, experiential expenditures on restaurant meals, health care, recreation, and education doubled over the same period from 17 percent of total spending to 34 percent.[31]

In keeping with this trend, the best hope for the reversal of economic polarization lies in the ongoing transformation of the personal services sector from low-end, low-skill scut work to up-market, high-skill professionalism. Tending to our homes, helping us improve and maintain our physical well-being, and taking care of us when we are sick and old—these are jobs that cannot be automated or outsourced, and so they promise to constitute an ever larger share of employment. And as we get richer, and spend ever more of our increased wealth on these kinds of services, it is virtually certain that competition will drive personal services industries toward ever higher quality. Which means an increasing demand for high-skill workers.

But the skills in demand here will differ from those of contemporary high-skill knowledge workers. "Book smarts," or critical thinking and complex communication skills, are not what is needed; rather, the demand will be for highly developed physical, interpersonal, and motivational skills. Recall that fluency with abstraction, which lies at the root of so much of what we call human capital, comes in three distinctive dimensions: intellectual abstraction, or analytical acuity; social abstraction, or "people skills"; and personal abstraction, or motivation and self-discipline. The rise of high-end personal services promises to boost the economic demand for the latter two dimensions of fluency—good news for people who, whatever their other aptitudes, are not well suited to schoolwork.

Unfortunately, the kinds of local, small-scale enterprises that will likely figure prominently in an upskilled personal-services sector must contend with a welter of regulatory obstacles. In particular, I want to focus on two main types: urban land use regulation and occupational licensing. Clearing away these barriers is an important step in the direction of a more inclusive, less polarized future.

As Ryan Avent has argued in his book *The Gated City*, NIMBYism and tightening restrictions on new building have pushed America's internal migration over the past two decades in perverse directions: away from the densest, most productive, innovative, and high-wage cities on the coasts and toward the sprawling, less productive, lower-wage ex-urbs of the Sunbelt. Avent calculates that the cost of this geographic misallocation of human capital runs somewhere between 0.25 percent and 0.5 percent of GDP every year.[32] In particular, artificially inflated rents discourage entrepreneurs from opening new businesses in the richest, most progressive markets—markets that should be acting as the seedbeds for the growth of high-value-added personal services. And of course, those markets aren't as large and rich as they otherwise could be because too many people are priced out of living there.

The requirement that you must get government permission before entering a particular line of work is a direct barrier to entrepreneurship—and one that has been growing rapidly in extent over the past few decades. In 1970, only about 10 percent of Americans worked in jobs subject to occupational licensing; today that figure stands at around 30 percent. Everybody is familiar with licensing requirements for doctors and lawyers. But similar requirements now apply in various states to librarians, upholsterers, massage therapists, cabinet makers, beekeepers, and fortune tellers. As of the early 1990s the Council of Governments estimated that more than eight hundred occupations were subject to licensing requirements in at least one state—a figure that has assuredly increased in the past two decades.

Licensing is defended on the ground of consumer protection, but the limited studies done of specific occupations show no improvement in the quality of services provided. Instead, the real effect of these restrictions seems to be simple protectionism. And on that score, licensing is highly effective: the best recent estimate shows that it is associated with an 18 percent increase in wages. The hike in pay is achieved by limiting the number of service providers: a comparison of occupations licensed in some states and not in others found that employment growth was 20 percent lower in states with restrictions. In other words, opportunities for would-be entrepreneurs are being systematically stifled. The exclusionary impact falls especially hard on non–college grads: 43 percent of people employed in licensed professions are legally required to get a college degree to ply their trade.[33]

Together these regulatory barriers are a major impediment to the emergence of new markets that could boost demand for a wide variety of non-IQ-centric human capital. With regard to land use, a big improvement over the status quo would be a move to price urban growth rather than banning it outright. In other words, instead of making new development subject to yes-or-no approval from city authorities, institute a system of exactions so that developers (and, ultimately, owners and tenants) internalize the costs of increased density.[34] Meanwhile, the legitimate consumer protection objectives of occupational licensing can be met satisfactorily with a system of voluntary certification. Service providers who met certification requirements could benefit from receiving an official seal of approval while leaving noncertified providers and their customers free to do business with each other.

Eight
What Lies Ahead

Enacting the reform agenda outlined in the previous chapter would help to spread the benefits of human capitalism much more broadly than they are at present. More effective early childhood interventions, greater competition in primary and secondary schooling, and an end to subsidizing high-cost, low-value higher education would lead to more widespread fluency with abstraction and thus higher levels of human capital throughout American society. Penal reform and prowork social policies could help to reduce social exclusion, encouraging productive participation in society and reducing the social pathologies that perpetuate disadvantages from generation to generation. And encouraging economic growth by dismantling barriers to entrepreneurship—in particular, reducing excessive land use restrictions and occupational licensing protectionism—would create more room at the top and encourage a healthy diversification of the kinds of high-skill labor valued in the marketplace.

Of course, the odds against all of these reforms being en-
acted anytime soon are somewhere between daunting and
astronomical. And even if, somehow, all of the formidable
political obstacles were overcome and this whole reform
agenda was implemented *in toto*, the effect would be far
from miraculous. Poverty would remain. Class divisions
would remain. Great differences in ability and opportunity
would remain. Such was the case, after all, even during the
relatively egalitarian decades of the mid-twentieth century.
Meanwhile, we are approaching the golden anniversary of
the War on Poverty. And after nearly a half century of concerted efforts to use public policy to combat entrenched socioeconomic disadvantage, the decidedly mixed results of
those efforts counsel against believing that transformative
success is just around the corner.

A quarter century ago, the sociologist Peter Rossi re-
flected on the disappointments of social reform in a paper
titled "The Iron Law of Evaluation and Other Metallic
Rules." Rossi was an expert in assessing the success or failure of social programs and, despite his strong progressive
leanings in favor of activist government, he recognized
that the high hopes that so often accompanied apparently
promising reforms were rarely vindicated. Thus his Iron
Law: "The expected value of any net impact assessment of
any large scale social program is zero." And, as an equally
depressing corollary, his Stainless Steel Law: "The better designed the impact assessment of a social program, the more
likely is the resulting estimate of net impact to be zero."[1]

Rossi was happy to admit that there were exceptions to
his laws, and that sometimes reform efforts could make a
positive difference. "But even in the case of successful so-

cial programs," he wrote, "the sizes of the net effects have not been spectacular. In the social program field, nothing has yet been invented which is as effective in its way as the smallpox vaccine was for the field of public health. In short, as is well known (and widely deplored) we are not on the verge of wiping out the social scourges of our time: ignorance, poverty, crime, dependency, or mental illness show great promise to be with us for some time to come."[2]

In the specific case of spurring more broad-based human capital development, there are ample grounds for modesty about the ultimate impact of reforms. The purpose of such reforms, after all, is to encourage cultural change, and thus to achieve anything they must overcome powerful forces of cultural inertia. Think about the persistence of cultural differences along regional, ethnic, or religious lines. Class-based cultural differences are no different. Yes, policy can influence cultural change, but sometimes cultural norms can resist any efforts to modify them. At the individual level, people with deeply ingrained beliefs, values, and habits will not relinquish them simply because some policy pushes in the other direction; instead, they will push back against the policy. That push-back is the source of the so-called law of unintended consequences: people have wills of their own and often refuse to act in the way that the well-intentioned policy planner wishes they would.

Consider the record of one eminently plausible reform idea that I did not include in my agenda: residential-mobility housing vouchers along the lines of the Department of Housing and Urban Development's trial Moving to Opportunity program. Under this program, residents of public housing could apply for special housing vouchers that permitted them to rent private units only in geographical areas with poverty rates under 10 percent. What happened to this experimental group after several years was then compared to another group that received normal housing vouchers without geographical restrictions and a control group of public housing residents that did receive vouchers at all.

The theory behind the Moving to Opportunity program was sound. Numerous studies have shown the deleterious effects of living in high-poverty areas—a result that is anything but surprising if you accept the cultural explanation of socioeconomic underachievement offered here. In such areas, the cultural influences that help to perpetuate disadvantage are basically undiluted and thus maximally potent. It makes sense, then, that deconcentrating poverty might help to break the cycle, as a poor kid growing up in a more affluent area will benefit from positive role models, helpful social networks, and the safety and stability that encourage the development of longer time horizons.

Yet when the follow-up studies were done, the results were keenly disappointing. Educational outcomes for the kids in the program showed no improvement, and neither did employment or earnings for the moms. While teenage girls did exhibit lower levels of risky behavior (drinking, smoking, taking drugs), teenage boys actually engaged in more risky behavior and were more likely to be arrested for crimes.

What happened? Even though families initially moved to low-poverty areas, most stayed in the same school districts and so there wasn't a big change in the educational opportunities afforded to the kids. Meanwhile, the program was a one-shot intervention, and in subsequent moves many families returned to their old or similar neighborhoods. In other words, program participants chose for understandable reason to stick with what they knew rather than take full advantage of the fresh start they had been offered.[3]

Such disappointments suggest that reforms might be more successful if they were just more intrusive. If people can be counted on to undermine the efficacy of interventions by doggedly persisting in their old ways of doing things, then the obvious response is tighten up the conditions for receiving program benefits. The fewer choices program participants are given, the fewer opportunities they will have to circumvent the program's intent and thus the better the odds for successful outcomes. Just stating such reasoning explicitly, however, should suffice to trigger moral alarm bells.

Here we encounter the old trade-off between equality and freedom—but in a new and unfamiliar context. Normally we think of this trade-off in terms of advancing equality by limiting the freedom of the rich and powerful—whether by taxing them to fund redistribution to the less well off, or regulating them to restrict their ability to take undue advantage of their superior position. Libertarians and progressives are usually at odds over making such trade-offs, as libertarians prioritize liberty while equality trumps for progressives. Taking their respective ideological positions comes all the more easily because of the fact that libertarians typically identify with society's high achievers (i.e., those paying the price of lost freedom) while progressives see themselves as champions of society's underdogs (i.e., those receiving the benefit of greater equality).

But here we are considering measures that promote equality by limiting the freedom of the disadvantaged. Now both the cost of reduced freedom and the benefit of improved equality fall on the same group of people. While libertarians should remain skeptical of greater government control over people's lives, now even progressives have cause to feel queasy. After all, we are talking about "helping" the poor by giving more power to the rich and powerful so they can run the poor's lives for their own good.

For the dismal asymptote toward which this kind of thinking tends, recall the tragic story of the "stolen generations" of Australian Aboriginal children. Between the beginning of the twentieth century and the end of the 1960s, somewhere between one-tenth and one-third of Aboriginal children were forcibly removed from their homes and raised in state- or church-run institutions or white foster homes. It is hard to conceive of a more radical attempt to effect cultural change by changing the environment in which kids are raised. And yet, despite the appallingly oppressive lengths to which Australian authorities were willing to go, this exercise in extreme social engineering ultimately came to naught: the terrible suffering imposed on children and parents alike led to no significant improvements in education or employment for the children removed from their homes.

We should therefore be modest, not just in our expectations for reform, but in our goals for reform as well. Policies constrained by proper respect for human rights and dignity will aspire to no more than incremental change. Their goal is to expose people to a different way of life; it cannot be to force them to take it.

This is a vitally important point. However squeamish we are about facing up to it, culture has a big impact on socioeconomic success—and thus cultural differences play a big role in explaining economic inequality. But we are uncomfortable acknowledging this truth precisely because we realize that a person's norms, beliefs, values, and habits are a constitutive part of her identity. And so, when we criticize cultural traits on the ground that they undercut socioeconomic achievement, we can't help but feel abashed that we are disrespecting people by denigrating things that matter to them on a deeply personal level.

Although I believe we need to get past our reticence and discuss cultural differences and their economic impacts forthrightly, that reticence does reflect healthy liberal instincts—namely, a respect for pluralism and a humble aversion to telling people that we know their true interests better than they do. Even if working-class culture is increasingly ill-suited to the demands of a highly complex modern economy, it is nonetheless the milieu in which real, flesh-and-blood people live good and decent lives. Love, laughter, family, and friends offer much more profound consolations for the human condition than do college degrees and high-paying jobs, and there is no reason to think that those great desiderata are in richer supply on the richer side of the class divide.

So in advocating policy reforms in order to effect cultural change, we need to refrain from the hubristic ambitions of social engineering. The idea of molding a "New Soviet Man" was an abomination; molding a New Capitalist Man is no better. Our goal must be the critical but fundamentally modest one of expanding people's choices—while recognizing and accepting that people may not end up choosing as we would.

None of this is to say that changes in public policy aren't needed, or that they are incapable of doing good. They are badly needed, and they could do a great deal of good. But they are hard to achieve, their effectiveness is always constrained by push-back and other sources of friction, and even their objectives must be limited by the very liberal values that lead us to worry about human capital inequality in the first place. So to be realistic, we should expect the future of human capitalism to be influenced more by the spontaneous, unplanned operation of broad social forces than by conscious, technocratic guidance from above.

Let's turn then from prescription to prediction. What are the plausible possibilities for the future direction of human capitalism?

Let's start with a prediction that can be ventured with great confidence: regardless of any progress in reducing intergenerational poverty and improving access to high-quality education, American society will continue to be characterized by wide variations in both ability and economic outcomes. Inequality is here to stay.

First of all, even if by magic we could erase all cultural differences that affect socioeconomic achievement, genes remain a potent and as yet immutable source of inequality. In chapter 5, I argued against what I called genetic fatalism—the idea that genes are so powerful in shaping socioeconomic destiny that changes in environment matter very little. I believe the evidence shows that childhood environment does have an important impact on adult outcomes, but I would never deny that genes are important too. Indeed, the paradoxical fact of the matter is that success in mitigating the environmental deficits that many children now face will only end up making genes even more important.

Think about two strains of plant, one of which naturally grows much taller than the other. Now mix the seeds together and plant them in a large plot. Parts of the plot get all the fertilizer, water, and sunlight the plants need to thrive, but in other parts of the plot one or more of these inputs are badly undersupplied. In this situation, environmental factors are going to vie with genetic factors in explaining the ultimate average height differences between the two strains. Some of the tall strain will be stunted by lack of water, fertilizer, or sunlight, while some of the short strain will grow to their maximum height under optimal conditions. By contrast, if all the plants in the plot receive all the inputs they need, the average height differences between the two strains at maturity will be explained entirely by the genetic differences between them.

Studies of genes' role in explaining IQ differences show a similar dynamic at work. According to research by the psychologist Eric Turkheimer and colleagues, the heritability of IQ—that is, the degree to which differences in IQ are attributable to genetic factors—varies dramatically by class. To reach this conclusion, they used the classic method of comparing IQ differences between identical and fraternal twins but then classified the twins according to their parents' education, occupation, and income. Among children of high socioeconomic status, they estimated heritability at 0.72; in other words, genetic factors accounted for 72 percent of variations of IQ. Shared environment, by contrast, could explain only 15 percent of IQ differences. Among low-socioeconomic-status kids, however, the relative importance of genes and environment was flipped: the estimate of heritability was only 0.10, while shared environment accounted for 58 percent of IQ variations.[4]

It's common sense, really: to the extent we reduce the nongenetic factors that produce differences in socioeconomic outcomes, the relative importance of genes in producing differences will grow. And genetic differences, by themselves, will ensure that wide variations in abilities and outcomes continue.

Differences in preferences are another ineradicable source of economic inequality. Some people care more about money than others; some people are more frugal and invest more wisely; some people put a higher value on work and career success relative to leisure and relationships. Such differences have been a major factor behind the rise of income inequality over the past generation. And, interestingly, any success in spurring a faster pace of human capital development will only increase the potency of this factor in generating income inequality.

The findings of the economist Thomas Lemieux are telling in this regard. The focus of this book has been on the rise what economists call "between-group" inequality: the growing differences in compensation between workers of different skill levels. But according to Lemieux, those differences account for only about a third of the overall increase in wage inequality since the early 1970s. The rest has been due to a rise in so-called within-group or residual inequality—that is, a wider range of wages among workers with the same education or experience. And looking at the period 1973–2003, Lemieux found that the entire increase in residual inequality during that time was attributable to "composition effects," or the changing demographics of the workforce.[5] American workers in 2003 were substantially older and better educated on average than their counterparts in 1973, and incomes tend to grow more unequal as people age and attend more school. The reasons aren't hard to understand: younger, less-educated workers are generally concentrated in low-paying jobs, while more experienced and better qualified workers have more options and thus can spread out all over the income scale depending on their preferences.

Consequently, if your goal is to compress the overall distribution of market compensation, you can't win for losing. If you want to reduce class-based or between-group inequality, you need to increase the supply of highly skilled workers and thereby drive down the wage premium they currently receive. But increasing the supply of highly skilled workers will end up boosting within-group inequality— and that's a far bigger deal in influencing the overall pattern of incomes.

Of course, here I am talking about the difficulty of reducing income inequality prior to taxes and transfers. So nothing I've said precludes the possibility of reducing final income inequality through hiking taxes on the rich and boosting transfers to the less well off. The much lower levels of income inequality experienced in western Europe, for example, are primarily due to such redistribution. Let's look at data on countries' Gini coefficients, the most comprehensive measure of income distribution. The scale goes from zero to one: a zero coefficient means that everybody in the country has the identical income, while a coefficient of one means that one person earns all the income in the country. When we look at Gini coefficients post taxes and transfers, inequality in the United States is much higher than in Europe: the coefficient for the United States is 0.38, as compared to 0.34 for Italy, 0.30 for Germany, 0.29 for France, and 0.26 for Sweden. But when we look at the situation prior to taxes and transfers, things appear very different: the United States scores 0.49, which is actually lower than Italy (0.53) and Germany (0.50) and only modestly higher than France (0.48) and Sweden (0.43).[6]

A move toward European-style redistribution, while effective in equalizing incomes, would leave unchanged the human capital inequality that is the focus of this book. Indeed, it would mask the human capital deficits that now plague American society and blunt the incentives for their remediation. To my way of thinking, the fact that large numbers of Americans lack the cognitive skills to thrive and flourish in the contemporary economy is a serious problem, whereas the mere fact that peoples' incomes vary widely for all sorts of reasons is not really a problem at all. So ramping up redistribution would solve a nonproblem while aggravating a real problem. No thanks.

In addition, and this is the decisive point, the welfare states of all the advanced countries, including the United States, are clearly fiscally unsustainable. Western Europe is presently in the midst of a gathering and potentially catastrophic debt crisis, and the paring back and restructuring of welfare benefits already under way is almost certain to continue. And the huge escalation of public debt in the United States in recent years is building political momentum here for scaling back the mounting liabilities of Social Security, Medicare, and Medicaid. For the foreseeable future, then, it seemly highly unlikely that the United States will implement the kinds of income-equalizing policies that are—for the time being at least—in place in western Europe.

There is thus no getting around it. As it has in the past, human capitalism will continue in the future to make us both smarter and more unequal in economic terms. But what about the specific dimension of inequality that has been the focus of this book—the class divide in fluency with abstraction? In other words, what are the prospects for the cultural polarization of recent decades to be reversed?

On the plus side, the economic incentives created by large pay differentials certainly push in the right direction. Perhaps, then, it is simply the case that they haven't yet had enough time to make their influence felt. After all, the widening of the income gap between the highly skilled and everybody else has been with us only for a generation or so. It could be that we are now in a period of temporary if uncomfortable disequilibrium in which social realities have raced ahead of cultural norms. As the huge impact that family and community life have on children's long-term futures becomes more widely understood, this cultural lag could begin to close on its own. Increasing numbers of parents who were not themselves raised in a culture of cognitive complexity may nonetheless do a better job of creating such a culture for their own kids.

And even without any major structural reforms, it's possible that social institutions outside the family will become much more effective in promoting human capital development and compensating for class-based disadvantages.

First of all, recent years have seen major breakthroughs in the scientific understanding of children's cognitive and psychological development as it pertains to socioeconomic achievement. That this book, which synthesizes some of these recent findings, is being published now is a testament both to what has been learned and the fact that it is not yet common knowledge. As this improved understanding diffuses through the social services and education sectors, the combined efforts of social programs and schools may finally start gaining traction in closing achievement gaps.

In addition, it's hard not to get excited about the transformative possibilities of online education. No doubt there is a great deal of hype, and many things that look promising now will turn out to be dead ends. Still, all caveats aside, the potential for revolutionizing teaching and learning looks genuine. In a world characterized by so much radical change, it is remarkable how much the classroom of today resembles that of decades, centuries, or even millennia past. But now, the very best instructors and highest-quality teaching materials can escape the narrow confines of the classroom and reach virtually everyone who wants access to them. And the cheapness of online dissemination is only the tip of the iceberg. Equally important is the capability for fine-grained, real-time monitoring of the learning process, which provides the data needed not only for immediate feedback to students but also for continuous improvement in instructional offerings. And the integration of online instruction with social media technologies allows for the creation of active, participatory communities of learners unbound by constraints of geography. Put all this together, and there is a chance that we are on the cusp of phenomenal improvements in the productivity and effectiveness of education—and commensurate gains in human capital development.

Although there are grounds for optimism, today's cultural polarization could well prove depressingly durable. For even though the relative economic standing of the working class has deteriorated in recent decades, in absolute terms material standards of living have continued to rise across the board. According to research from the Brookings Institution, more than four-fifths of forty-year-old Americans live in households with higher real per capita family incomes than their parents did at the same age.[7] And indeed, measuring gains in terms of real (i.e., inflation-adjusted) incomes understates the good news. First, adjustments for inflation can never fully capture the gains in standard of living made possible by the introduction of new products: no matter how much money you made in the early 1970s, you could not surf the Internet or use an ATM or listen to an iPod or take ibuprofen for a headache or get an MRI if the headache persisted. Furthermore, calculations of real income are always made on the basis of a single monolithic estimate of inflation. But it turns out that the prices of high-end consumer goods have been rising much faster than those of low-end goods, and thus the inflation rate for the poor has been lower than that for the rich.[8] Which means, in turn, that conventional estimates understate the true gains made by the poor in terms of material standard of living.

Look, for example, at a comparison of all households in 1971 to households *below the poverty line* in 1994. Some 72 percent of poor households had washing machines in 1994, compared to 71 percent of all households in 1971; 50 percent had clothes dryers, while only 45 percent of all households had them in the early 1970s; 98 percent had refrigerators, up from 83 percent of all households a couple of decades earlier; 93 percent had color televisions, a dramatic increase over the 43 percent figure for all households in 1971; 50 percent had air conditioners, as opposed to 32 percent of all households earlier; and 60 percent had microwave ovens, while fewer than 1 percent of all households had one in 1971.[9] In some important respects, then, poor Americans have a higher standard of living than average Americans did a generation ago.

Why does all of this matter? Because it means that the material consequences of socioeconomic underachievement are growing ever less severe. Of course it is fundamentally good news that the material circumstances of the least well off are improving. But there is a downside: just as downward relative mobility sharpens the incentives to work hard, amass human capital, and get ahead, upward absolute mobility dulls those incentives. It is a grim, uncomfortable fact that the lash of material hardship is a powerful motivator. If living conditions for those in the bottom half are decently comfortable, the motivation to expend the effort needed to move upward will have to come from elsewhere. And it might not come at all.

This dynamic is especially apparent in the declining labor-force participation rate for low-skill workers. Back in 1968, only about 4 percent of white men ages thirty to forty-nine with a high school diploma or less were out of the workforce; by 2008, that figure had climbed to 12 percent.[10] It is particularly interesting to compare low-skill workers from different ethnic backgrounds. As of 2010, 71 percent of Hispanics (male and female) with less than a high school diploma were in the workforce, compared to only 48 percent of whites and 39 percent of African Americans. Why is the work ethic so much stronger among low-skill Hispanics? Many Hispanics, of course, are either immigrants from less developed countries or the children of such immigrants, and thus their attitudes about work are shaped by relatively recent experience of serious material deprivation. By contrast, native-born Americans are raised in a society where the alternative to work is fairly reliable state provision of basic material needs. Working hard for low pay and little security looks less attractive to them, not surprisingly.

Many libertarians will blame this decline in the work ethic on the welfare state. And they have a point: from the old Aid to Families with Dependent Children to today's Social Security Disability Insurance, government programs to aid the needy have regularly featured perverse incentives that discourage work. But the fundamental problem lies, not in the design of any particular program, but in rising living standards. Even if the welfare state were somehow eliminated and all assistance for people in need came from private charity, the same dynamic would continue to operate. As a society grows richer, the prevailing conceptions of poverty and need will be ratcheted upward. In other words, what is thought to be the minimum decent standard of living in that society will rise in step with rising overall living standards. And as the social minimum approaches the market value of particular people's labor, those people will face increasingly strong incentives to drop out of the workforce.

The two major economic factors—downward relative mobility and upward absolute mobility—thus push in op-

posing directions. Consequently, the future of human capitalism may well hinge on the relative strength of these factors in motivating the middling and lower ranks of society.
The sting of lower social status provides impetus for the
greater development of talents, while the lull of rising material comfort encourages a complacent acceptance of the
path of least resistance. Which effect will be more powerful?
It is worth pausing a moment to consider the irony inher-
ent in this state of affairs. Progressives, who typically identify with society's underdogs, presumably root for a world
in which the less advantaged are lifted up and enjoy more
of the blessings that are currently the preserve of an elite
minority. At the same time, however, progressives tend to
decry the jockeying for relative social position that, in this
case at least, could lead to more broadly shared opportunities. And progressives generally favor greater downward
redistribution of income, even though ameliorating the
material consequences of socioeconomic underachievement could end up rendering higher achievement levels
less likely.

In the end, though, I doubt that the clash of economic
incentives will prove decisive one way or the other. They
push in opposite directions and thus may well cancel each
other out—or at least render the net effect one way or another of little account. So if external motivations of material
gain and relative status turn out to be inconclusive, what
ultimately will matter is the strength of purely internal, personal motivations. Specifically, is the intrinsic appeal of developing one's capabilities and enjoying the productive exercise thereof sufficiently strong and broad-based to induce
the necessary effort?

Here we arrive at the crux of the matter. When people are freed from the yoke of real or perceived economic necessity, how will they choose to live? In his wonderful and prescient 1930 essay "The Economic Possibilities for Our Grandchildren," John Maynard Keynes framed the issue aptly. Writing in the depths of the Great Depression, Keynes confidently asserted that the terrible dislocations of his day were just a temporary reversal in the march of economic progress. And he foresaw that such progress was leading humanity in ever-increasing numbers toward a predicament both enviable and fateful. "Thus for the first time since his creation," Keynes wrote, "man will be faced with his real, his permanent problem—how to use his freedom from pressing economic cares, how to occupy the leisure, which science and compound interest will have won for him, to live wisely and agreeably and well."[11]

Rising levels of human capital throughout society have been an essential ingredient in bringing us to the point where this problem is coming into view. Two possible futures loom. In one, the allure of self-development will lead the broad run of society to meet the great and abiding challenge of "living wisely and agreeably and well." In the other, a minority flush with human capital will thrive and flourish while the majority content themselves with bread and circuses.

Which future awaits? However things turn out, it appears that fundamental facts about human nature will be revealed. Optimists and pessimists may place their bets accordingly.

Notes

Introduction

1. Of course, as society grows more complex, many particular aspects of life are dramatically simplified. Recall Alfred North Whitehead's observation, "Civilization advances by extending the number of important operations which we can perform without thinking of them." To take just one example, finding one's way in a car used to involve poring over maps, asking for directions when lost, and so on, whereas now GPS technology allows us to type in an address and then just do as we're told. Yet life overall has grown more complex in two important ways. First, as I will describe later, work generally involves much more complex tasks than it once did. And second, life now presents us with far more choices than before—from where to live, what career to pursue, and whom to make friends with all the way down to which of the dozens of different breakfast cereals to purchase in the grocery store.

2. Brink Lindsey, *The Age of Abundance: How Prosperity Transformed America's Politics and Culture* (New York: Collins, 2007).

3. To avoid or at least minimize confusion, let me offer here a brief note on terminology. Throughout this book I will use the term *human capital* expansively to include what sociologists call *cultural capital* (cultural knowledge that confers socioeconomic status) and *social capital* (economically valuable social networks). Scholars who distinguish among these forms of capital may object, but in my analysis the concepts are so interrelated that drawing distinctions merely clutters rather than clarifies. Specifically, my argument here is that the most important forms of human capital are all cultural capital (i.e., they are transmitted culturally through families and communities), and that one particular dimension of this cultural capital (which I refer to as fluency with social abstraction) consists of the capacity to amass social capital.

■ **Chapter One: The Rise of Complexity**

1. Peter Lyman and Hal R. Varian, *How Much Information 2003*, http://chnm.gmu.edu/digitalhistory/links/pdf/preserving /8_5a.pdf.

2. Gregory Clark, *A Farewell to Alms: A Brief Economic History of the World* (Princeton, N.J.: Princeton University Press, 2007), pp. 1–2.

3. Douglass C. North, *Structure and Change in Economic History* (New York: W. W. Norton, 1981), pp. 158–186.

4. Clark, *A Farewell to Alms*, p. 140.

■ **Chapter Two: The Abstract Art of Modern Living**

1. See Robin Dunbar, *How Many Friends Does One Person Need? Dunbar's Number and Other Evolutionary Quirks* (Cambridge, Mass.: Harvard University Press, 2010).

2. Thomas K. Landauer, "How Much Do People Remember? Some Estimates of the Quantity of Learned Information

in Long-Term Memory," *Cognitive Science* 10, no. 4 (October–December 1986): 477–493.

3. See Douglas S. Massey, *Strangers in a Strange Land, Humans in an Urbanizing World* (New York: W. W. Norton, 2005), pp. 187–188; United Nations Educational, Scientific, and Cultural Organization, *The Global Literacy Challenge: A Profile of Youth and Adult Literacy at the Midpoint of the United Nations Literacy Decade 2003–2012,* 2008, http://unesdoc.unesco.org/images/0016/001631/163170e.pdf.

4. Clark, *A Farewell to Alms,* pp. 177–178, 186.

5. James R. Flynn, *What Is Intelligence?* (New York: Cambridge University Press, 2007), p. 25.

6. Ulrich Neisser, "Rising Scores on Intelligence Tests," *American Scientist,* September–October 1997, http://www.americanscientist.org/issues/feature/rising-scores-on-intelligence-tests/1.

7. Lawrence H. Keeley, *War before Civilization: The Myth of the Peaceful Savage* (New York: Oxford University Press, 1997).

8. Edward C. Banfield, *The Moral Basis of a Backward Society* (New York: Free Press, 1958), p. 83.

9. See Rose Laub Coser, *In Defense of Modernity: Role Complexity and Individual Autonomy* (Palo Alto, Calif.: Stanford University Press, 1991).

10. Banfield, *The Moral Basis of a Backward Society,* p. 77.

11. Clark, *A Farewell to Alms,* pp 168–175.

▪ Chapter Three: Capitalism with a Human Face

1. Gary S. Becker, "The Age of Human Capital," in *Education in the Twenty-first Century,* ed. Edward P. Lazear (Stanford, Calif.: Hoover Institution Press, 2002), p. 3.

2. See Richard E. Nisbett, *Intelligence and How to Get It: Why School and Cultures Count* (New York: W. W. Norton, 2009), p. 5.

3. See Stephen V. Cameron and James J. Heckman, "The Nonequivalence of High School Equivalents," *Journal of Labor Economics* 11, no. 1, part 1 (January 1993): 1–47.

4. See Gary S. Becker and Kevin M. Murphy, "The Upside of Inequality," *The American*, May/June 2007, http://www.american.com/archive/2007/may-june-magazine-contents/the-upside-of-income-inequality.

5. David T. Ellwood and Christopher Jencks, "The Spread of Single-Parent Families in the United States since 1960," Kennedy School of Government Faculty ResearchWorking Paper no. RWP04-008, February 2004, table 2.9, http://web.hks.harvard.edu/publications/workingpapers/citation.aspx?PubId=2069.

6. For useful data on benefits associated with earning a college degree, see College Board Advocacy and Policy Center, "Education Pays 2010: The Benefits of Higher Education for Individuals and Society," http://trends.collegeboard.org/downloads/Education_Pays_2010.pdf.

7. Frank H. Knight, *Risk, Uncertainty and Profit* (New York: Houghton Mifflin, 1921), pp. 268–269.

■ Chapter Four: Class and Consciousness

1. Herbert J. Gans, *The Urban Villagers: Group and Class in the Life of Italian-Americans* (New York: Free Press, 1962), p. 121.

2. Annette Lareau, *Unequal Childhoods: Class, Race, and Family Life* (Berkeley: University of California Press, 2003), pp. 242–243.

3. Gans, *The Urban Villagers*, p. 90.

4. Ibid., p. 93.

5. See Basil Bernstein, *Class, Codes and Control: Theoretical Studies toward a Sociology of Language* (London: Routledge & Kegan Paul, 1971).

6. Lareau, *Unequal Childhoods*, pp. 107, 146.

7. See Samuel Bowles and Herbert Gintis, "The Inheritance of Inequality," *Journal of Economic Perspectives* 16, no. 3 (Summer 2002): 3–30.

8. See Julia B. Isaacs, "Economic Mobility of Families across Generations," in *Getting Ahead or Losing Ground: Economic*

Mobility in America, by Julia B. Isaacs, Isabel V. Sawhill, and Ron Haskins, February 2008, p. 19, http://www.economicmobility .org/assets/pdfs/PEW_EMP_GETTING_AHEAD_FULL.pdf.

9. Malcolm Gladwell: *Outliers: The Story of Success* (New York: Little, Brown, 2008), pp. 35–68.

10. Betty Hart and Todd R. Risley, "The Early Catastrophe: The 30 Million Word Gap by Age 3," *American Educator* 1, no. 1 (Spring 2003): 4–9.

11. Lareau, *Unequal Childhoods,* pp. 2, 3.

12. Judith Rich Harris, *The Nurture Assumption: Why Children Turn Out the Way They Do* (New York: Touchstone, 1998).

13. See Douglas S. Massey, *Categorically Unequal: The American Stratification System* (New York: Russell Sage Foundation, 2007).

14. Roland G. Fryer, "Acting White," *Education Next,* Winter 2006, http://www.economics.harvard.edu/faculty/fryer/files /aw_ednext.pdf.

■ **Chapter Five: Inequality as a Culture Gap**

1. See Richard J. Herrnstein and Charles Murray, *The Bell Curve: Intelligence and Class Structure in American Life* (New York: Free Press, 1996). Note that in his most recent book, Murray focuses on cultural rather than genetic factors in explaining the growth of class divisions along educational lines—in particular, attitudes toward marriage, work, and religion. See Charles Murray, *Coming Apart: The State of White America, 1960–2010* (New York: Crown Forum, 2012). I will discuss his cultural analysis later in the book.

2. Angela L. Duckworth and Martin E. P. Seligman, "Self-Discipline Outdoes IQ in Predicting Academic Performance of Adolescents," *Psychological Science* 16, no. 12 (2005): 939–944.

3. Bowles and Gintis, "The Inheritance of Inequality."

4. See Nisbett, *Intelligence and How to Get It,* pp. 24–25.

5. See ibid., pp. 29–30; Mike Stoolmiller, "Implications of the Restricted Range of Family Environments for Estimates of

Heritability and Nonshared Environment in Behavior–Genetic Adoption Studies," *Psychological Bulletin* 125, no. 4 (July 1999): 392–409.

6. See Nisbett, *Intelligence and How to Get It*, pp. 32–34.

7. See James J. Heckman and Alan B. Krueger, *Inequality in America: What Role for Human Capital Policies?* (Cambridge, Mass.: MIT Press, 2005), p. 100.

8. See Anne E. Cunningham and Keith E. Stanovich, "What Reading Does for the Mind," *American Educator* 22, no. 1–2 (Spring/Summer 1998): 8–15.

9. See, e.g., Jere R. Behrman and Paul Taubman, "Is Schooling Mostly 'in the Genes'? Nature–Nurture Decomposition Using Data on Relatives," *Journal of Political Economy* 97, no. 6 (December 1989): 1425–1446 ("88 percent of the variation in schooling arises from genetic variations"); Bruce Sacerdote, "What Happens When We Randomly Assign Children to Families?" National Bureau of Economic Research Working Paper no. 10894, November 2004 (no correlation between incomes of children and adoptive parents).

10. See Anders Björklund, Markus Jäntti, and Gary Solon, "Influences of Nature and Nurture on Earnings Variation: A Report on a Study of Various Sibling Types in Sweden," in *Unequal Chances: Family Background and Economic Success*, by Samuel Bowles, Herbert Gintis, and Melissa Osborne Groves (New York: Russell Sage Foundation, 2005), pp. 145–164.

11. See Paul Miller, Charles Mulvey, and Nick Martin, "Genetic and Environmental Contributions to Educational Attainment in Australia," *Economics of Education Review* 20 (2001): 211–224.

12. Christopher Jencks and Laura Tach, "Would Equal Opportunity Mean More Mobility?" John F. Kennedy School of Government Faculty Research Working Paper RWP05-037, May 2005.

13. Bowles and Gintis, "The Inheritance of Inequality."

14. Bruce Sacerdote, "Nature and Nurture Effects on Children's Outcomes: What Have We Learned from Studies of Twins

and Adoptees?" working paper, February 27, 2008, http://www
.econ.nyu.edu/user/bisina/Chapter5_Sacerdote.pdf.

15. Nisbett, *Intelligence and How to Get It*, p. 36.

16. James P. Smith, "Assimilation across the Latino Generations," *American Economic Review* 93, no. 2 (2003): 315–319.

17. George J. Borjas, "Making It in America: Social Mobility
in the Immigrant Population," National Bureau of Economic
Research Working Paper no. 12088, March 2006.

18. For a typical example of this attitude, see Paul Krugman,
"Blaming the Victims of Inequality," *New York Times*, February 7,
2012, http://krugman.blogs.nytimes.com/2012/02/07/blaming
-the-victims-of-inequality/.

19. Susan E. Mayer, *What Money Can't Buy: Family Income
and Children's Life Chances* (Cambridge, Mass.: Harvard University Press, 1998), p. 12. Emphasis is in the original.

▪ Chapter Six: From Convergence to Polarization

1. Gary Burtless and Christopher Jencks, "American Inequal-
ity and Its Consequences," in *Agenda for the Nation*, ed. Henry
Aaron, James Lindsay, and Pietro Nivola (Washington, D.C.:
Brookings Institution Press, 2003), p. 65, fig. 3-2.

2. For this turn of phrase, see Bennett Harrison and Barry
Bluestone, *The Great U-Turn: Corporate Restructuring and the
Polarizing of America* (New York: Basic Books, 1988).

3. Burtless and Jencks, "American Inequality and Its
Consequences."

4. See Becker and Murphy, "The Upside of Inequality."

5. See, e.g., David Autor, "The Polarization of Job Opportunities in the U.S. Labor Market: Implications for Employment
and Earnings," paper jointly released by the Center for American
Progress and the Hamilton Project, April 2010, http://econ-www
.mit.edu/files/5554.

6. See Frank Levy and Richard J. Murnane, *The New Division of Labor: How Computers Are Creating the Next Job Market* (Princeton, N.J.: Princeton University Press, 2005).

7. See James J. Heckman and Paul A. LaFontaine, "The American High School Graduation Rate: Trends and Levels," Institute for the Study of Labor Discussion Paper no. 3216, December 2007.

8. See Claudia Goldin and Lawrence Katz, *The Race between Education and Technology* (Cambridge, Mass.: Belknap Press of Harvard University Press, 2008), p. 297, table 8.1.

9. James J. Heckman and Dimitry V. Masterov, "The Productivity Argument for Investing in Young Children," National Bureau of Economic Research Working Paper no. 13016, April 2007.

10. Steven P. Martin, "Growing Evidence for a 'Divorce Divide'? Education and Marital Dissolution Rates in the U.S. since the 1970s," Russell Sage Foundation Working Paper, 2004.

11. Steven P. Martin, "Growing Evidence for a 'Divorce Divide'? Education and Marital Dissolution Rates in the United States," undated PowerPoint presentation, http://www.bsos.umd.edu/socy/smartin/reviews/smartin_opr.ppt.

12. Suzanne Bianchi, John P. Robinson, and Melissa A. Milkie, *Changing Rhythms of American Family Life* (New York: Russell Sage Foundation Publications, 2007).

13. Garey Ramey and Valerie A. Ramey, "The Rug Rat Race," in *Brookings Papers on Economic Activity: Spring 2010*, ed. David H. Romer and Justin Wolfers (Washington, D.C.: Brookings Institution, 2010), pp. 129–176. Note that the Rameys define time spent with children differently than the authors of the previous study do.

14. Lareau, *Unequal Childhoods*, p. 238 (emphasis added).

15. Lindsey, *The Age of Abundance*.

16. See Ronald Inglehart and Christian Welzel, *Modernization, Cultural Change, and Democracy: The Human Development Sequence* (New York: Cambridge University Press, 2005).

17. Murray, *Coming Apart*, p. 291.

■ **Chapter Seven: Reforming Human Capitalism**

1. Quoted in Lawrence E. Harrison, *The Central Liberal Truth: How Politics Can Change a Culture and Save It from Itself* (New York: Oxford University Press, 2006).

2. Furthermore, the evidence suggests that as economies grow richer and more advanced, they become increasingly dependent on innovation to sustain continued growth. See Brink Lindsey, "Frontier Economics: Why Entrepreneurial Capitalism Is Needed Now More Than Ever," Kauffman Foundation Research Series on Dynamics of Economic Growth, April 2011, http://www.kauffman.org/uploadedFiles/frontier_economics_4_06.pdf.

3. John Haltiwanger, "Job Creation and Firm Dynamics in the U.S.," National Bureau of Economic Research, May 2011, http://www.nber.org/chapters/c12451.pdf.

4. See Kauffman Task Force on Law, Innovation, and Growth, *Rules for Growth: Promoting Innovation and Growth through Legal Reform* (Kansas City, Mo.: Kauffman Foundation, 2011); William J. Baumol, Robert E. Litan, and Carl J. Schramm, *Good Capitalism, Bad Capitalism, and the Economics of Growth and Prosperity* (New Haven, Conn.: Yale University Press, 2009).

5. Christopher Berry, "School District Consolidation and Student Outcomes: Does Size Matter?" paper prepared for the conference "School Board Politics," Kennedy School of Government, Harvard University, October 15–17, 2003.

6. Frederick M. Hess, "Does School Choice 'Work'?" *National Affairs*, Fall 2010, http://www.nationalaffairs.com/publications/detail/does-school-choice-work.

7. See Vilsa E. Curto, Roland G. Fryer Jr., and Meghan L. Howard, "It May Not Take a Village: Increasing Achievement among the Poor," in *Social Inequality and Educational Disadvantage* (Washington, D.C.: Brookings Institution Press, forthcoming), http://www.economics.harvard.edu/faculty/fryer/files/SIED_1-21-11.pdf.

8. U.S. Department of Health and Human Services, Administration for Children and Families, *Head Start Impact Study Final Report*, January 2010, http://www.acf.hhs.gov/programs/opre/hs/impact_study/reports/impact_study/executive_summary_final.pdf.

9. Will Dobbie and Roland G. Fryer Jr., "Are High-Quality Schools Enough to Increase Achievement among the Poor? Evidence from the Harlem Children's Zone," *American Economic Journal: Applied Economics* 3, no. 3 (2011): 158–187.

10. James J. Heckman, Syong Hyeok Moon, Rodrigo Pinto, Peter Savelyev, and Adam Yavitz, "A New Cost–Benefit and Rate of Return Analysis for the Perry Preschool Program: A Summary," Institute for the Study of Labor Policy Paper no. 17, July 2010, http://ftp.iza.org/pp17.pdf.

11. See Douglas Clement, "Interview with James Heckman," *The Region*, Federal Reserve Bank of Minneapolis, June 1, 2005, http://www.minneapolisfed.org/publications_papers/pub_display.cfm?id=3278.

12. See Edmund S. Phelps, *Rewarding Work: How to Restore Participation and Self-Support to Free Enterprise* (Cambridge, Mass.: Harvard University Press, 1997).

13. David Autor, "The Unsustainable Rise of the Disability Rolls in the United States: Causes, Consequences, and Policy Options," National Bureau of Economic Research Working Paper no. 17697, December 2011; Richard V. Burkhauser and Mary C. Daly, *The Declining Work and Welfare of People with Disabilities: What Went Wrong and a Strategy for Change* (Washington, D.C.: American Enterprise Institute, 2011); Richard V. Burkhauser, "A Proposal for Fundamental Change in Social Security Disability Insurance," Statement before the House Committee on Ways and Means Subcommittee on Social Security, September 14, 2012, http://waysandmeans.house.gov/uploaded files/burkhauser_testimony_ss914.pdf.

14. David Cole, "Turning the Corner on Mass Incarceration?" *Ohio State Journal of Criminal Law* 9, no. 1 (2011): 27–51.

15. John J. DiIulio Jr., "Rethinking Crime—Again," *Democracy: A Journal of Ideas*, Spring 2010, http://www .democracyjournal.org/16/6739.php?page=all.

16. Ibid.

17. See Mark A. R. Kleiman, *When Brute Force Fails: How to Have Less Crime and Less Punishment* (Princeton, N.J.: Princeton University Press, 2009).

18. Mark A. R. Kleiman, "Jail Break: How Smarter Parole and Probation Can Cut the Nation's Incarceration Rate," *Washington Monthly*, July/August 2009, pp. 56–60.

19. See Ben Wildavsky, *The Great Brain Race: How Global Universities Are Reshaping the World* (Princeton, N.J.: Princeton University Press, 2010).

20. Richard Arum and Josipa Roksa, *Academically Adrift: Limited Learning on College Campuses* (Chicago: University of Chicago Press, 2011), p. 30.

21. Ibid., pp. 35–36.

22. See Alexander W. Astin, "In 'Academically Adrift,' Data Don't Back Up Sweeping Claim," *Chronicle of Higher Education*, February 14, 2011.

23. Arum and Roksa, *Academically Adrift*, pp. 3, 71.

24. Catherine Rampell, "The College Majors That Do Best in the Job Market," *New York Times*, May 19, 2011, http://economix .blogs.nytimes.com/2011/05/19/the-college-majors-that-do-best -in-the-job-market/.

25. National Center for Education Statistics, http://nces.ed.gov/ programs/coe/tables/table-trc-3.asp.

26. See Alex Tabarrok, "College Has Been Oversold," in *Launching the Innovation Renaissance: A New Path to Bring Smart Ideas to Market Fast* (TED Books, Kindle edition, November 21, 2011).

27. National Center for Education Statistics, http://nces.ed .gov/fastfacts/display.asp?id=76.

28. See Tamar Lewin, "College Graduates' Debt Burden Grew, Yet Again, in 2010," *New York Times*, November 2, 2011, http://

www.nytimes.com/2011/11/03/education/average-student-loan
-debt-grew-by-5-percent-in-2010.html.

29. See, e.g., Stephanie Rieg Cellini and Claudia Goldin, "Does Federal Student Aid Raise Tuition? New Evidence on For-Profit Colleges," National Bureau of Economic Research Working Paper no. 17827, February 2012.

30. See Kevin Carey, "A Radical Solution for America's Worsening College Tuition Bubble," *New Republic*, January 10, 2012, http://www.tnr.com/article/politics/99415/college-tuition-afford-higher-education.

31. See Virginia Postrel, *The Substance of Style: How the Rise of Aesthetic Value Is Remaking Commerce, Culture, and Consciousness* (New York: Harper, 2003).

32. Ryan Avent, *The Gated City* (Amazon Digital Services, Kindle Edition, 2011). See also Matthew Yglesias, *The Rent Is Too Damn High* (New York: Simon & Schuster, 2012).

33. Morris M. Kleiner, "Occupational Licensing: Protecting the Public Interest or Protectionism?" W. E. Upjohn Institute for Employment Research, Policy Paper no. 2011-009, 2011; Morris M. Kleiner and Alan B. Krueger, "Analyzing the Extent and Influence of Occupational Licensing on the Labor Market," Institute for the Study of Labor Discussion Paper no. 5505, February 2011.

34. See Nicole Garnett, "Land Use Regulation, Innovation, and Growth," in Kauffman Task Force on Law, Innovation, and Growth, *Rules for Growth*, pp. 286–312.

■ **Chapter Eight: What Lies Ahead**

1. Peter Rossi, "The Iron Law of Evaluation and Other Metallic Rules," *Research in Social Problems and Public Policy* 4 (1987): 4.

2. Ibid., p. 6.

3. See, e.g., Stefanie DeLuca, "Neighborhood Matters," *Boston Review*, January/February 2008; William A. V. Clark, "Reexamining the Moving to Opportunity Study and Its Contribution

to Changing the Distribution of Poverty and Ethnic Concentration," *Demography* 45, no. 3 (2008): 515–535.

4. Eric Turkheimer, Andreanna Haley, Mary Waldron, Brian D'Onofrio, and Irving I. Gottesman, "Socioeconomic Status Modifies Heritability of IQ in Young Children," *Psychological Science* 14, no. 6 (November 2003): 623–638.

5. Thomas Lemieux, "Increasing Residual Wage Inequality: Composition Effects, Noisy Data, or Rising Demand for Skill?" *American Economic Review* 96, no. 3 (June 2006): 461–498.

6. Statistics from the Organisation for Economic Co-operation and Development for the late 2000s, http://stats.oecd.org.

7. See Isaacs, "Economic Mobility of Families across Generations," p. 22 n. 5.

8. See Christian Broda and John Romalis, "The Welfare Implications of Rising Price Dispersion," working paper, July 4, 2009, http://faculty.chicagobooth.edu/john.romalis/Research/Draft_v7.pdf.

9. W. Michael Cox and Richard Alm, *Myths of Rich and Poor: Why We're Better Off Than We Think* (New York: Basic Books, 1999), p. 15, table 1.2.

10. Murray, *Coming Apart*, pp. 173–174.

11. John Maynard Keynes, *Essays in Persuasion* (New York: W. W. Norton & Company, 1963), pp. 358–374.

Index